Y0-DXG-788

Promoting
POSITIVE
Behaviors

Dedicated to all the teachers and principals throughout time whose insights and focus on the little things enable today's educators to artistically manage students and schools and achieve outstanding results.

Promoting
POSITIVE
Behaviors

An Elementary Principal's Guide to Structuring the Learning Environment

PAUL G. YOUNG

Foreword by Gail Connelly

Executive Director, National Association of Elementary School Principals

A JOINT PUBLICATION

CORWIN PRESS
A SAGE Company
Thousand Oaks, CA 91320

NATIONAL ASSOCIATION OF ELEMENTARY SCHOOL PRINCIPALS
Serving All Elementary and Middle Level Principals

For information:

Corwin Press
A SAGE Company
2455 Teller Road
Thousand Oaks, California 91320
www.corwinpress.com

SAGE Ltd.
1 Oliver's Yard
55 City Road
London EC1Y 1SP
United Kingdom

SAGE India Pvt. Ltd.
B 1/I 1 Mohan Cooperative
    Industrial Area
Mathura Road, New Delhi 110 044
India

SAGE Asia-Pacific Pte. Ltd.
33 Pekin Street #02-01
Far East Square
Singapore 048763

Printed in the United States of America.

Library of Congress Cataloging-in-Publication Data

Young, Paul G., 1950-
Promoting positive behaviors : an elementary principal's guide to structuring the learning environment / Paul G. Young.
      p. cm.
Includes bibliographical references and index.
ISBN 978-1-4129-5303-0 (cloth)
ISBN 978-1-4129-5304-7 (pbk.)
   1. School discipline—United States—Handbooks, manuals, etc. 2. School management and organization—United States—Handbooks, manuals, etc. 3. School principals—United States—Handbooks, manuals, etc. I. Title.

LB3012.2.Y68 2008
371.5—dc22   2007031651

This book is printed on acid-free paper.

07   08   09   10   11   10 9 8 7 6 5 4 3 2 1

Acquisitions Editor:	Jean Ward
Managing Editor:	Debra Stollenwerk
Editorial Assistants:	Jordan Barbakow, Allison Scott
Production Editor:	Libby Larson
Copy Editor:	Teresa Herlinger
Typesetter:	C&M Digitals (P) Ltd.
Proofreader:	Theresa Kay
Indexer:	Michael Ferreira
Cover Designer:	Michael Dubowe
Graphic Designer:	Monique Hahn

Contents

Foreword

The underachievement of our nation's schoolchildren has been documented for more than a decade in the public media and professional literature. Many policymakers, educators, and writers focus on students' increasing lack of readiness skills, disengaged parents, and society's malaise toward public education as factors contributing to poor academic performance. Without a doubt, those are realities that educators face every day. No one understands this more than Paul Young, who is a veteran principal and current thought leader on primary education. *Promoting Positive Behaviors: An Elementary Principal's Guide to Structuring the Learning Environment* addresses the many benefits of a well-structured school and provides educators with valuable lessons to identify, understand, and capitalize on their strengths to positively shape school structure and to improve teaching and learning. As you'll discover in this reflective book, Paul Young offers some commonsense recommendations for the adults in schools, which when consistently implemented reinforce and support the structure of each routine day as well as the entire school year. They promote positive behaviors that will increase instructional time—and make the school a better place to be for both students and adults.

Every principal should take time to reflect on the advice and ideas contained within this book. Paul Young is a former president of the National Association of Elementary School Principals (NAESP), a nationally trained mentor with the Peer Assisted Leadership Services (PALS) program, and a strong advocate for children. He has mentored numerous principals and coordinated the NAESP Principals' HelpLine, helping practitioners develop into capable building managers and instructional leaders. With this book, his advice will help each reader become a stronger and more confident *leader*.

The suggestions in this book will remain constant with time. You will gather many ideas when you read it straight through, and you can refer back to it often for reflection on various topics. Use it as a tool for staff development and leadership development. Our members and principals throughout the world will benefit from the insights of this respected leader. The children in our schools will benefit from a structured environment in which positive behaviors of both adults and students lead to high levels of achievement and satisfaction with learning.

Gail Connelly
Executive Director
National Association of Elementary School Principals

Acknowledgments

From my days attending elementary school, I have been fortunate to be a student and observer of many master teachers. Without exception, these individuals were positive role models and superbly organized, team players—leaders among their peers. I acknowledge that many of the insights and stories in this book are included as a tribute to them.

As a principal, I was fortunate to meet leaders of all types of schools throughout the nation. Whenever possible, I listened to presentations of best practices by distinguished leaders or observed in their schools for a firsthand look. It is with sincere gratitude that I thank them for willingly sharing their beliefs about school structure and organizational procedures. The ideas shared in this book have been affirmed by observing what others have or have not done to achieve success.

Particularly, I acknowledge some special, critical friends for the time spent discussing their ideas related to this book. Included among them are C. Lynn Babcock, Caroline Borrow, Marcia Brueggen, Larry Burgess, Scott Ebbrecht, Rob Libbee, Jeromey Sheets, Jonn and Sue Ellen Simmons, June Slobodian, and Steve Zinser.

I especially thank the acquisitions editors at Corwin Press, Jean Ward, Hudson Perigo, and Debra Stollenwerk, for their encouragement, guidance, and support. Their thoughtful insights and comments were vital as this book progressed through various stages of development.

Special thanks to my wife, Gertrude, and daughters Katie and Mary Ellen, without whose support any ventures such as this would be impossible.

Corwin Press would like to thank the following individuals for their contributions:

Jerry Vaughn
Middle School Principal
Cabot Public Schools
Cabot, AR

Michelle Kocar
Principal
Avon Heritage South Elementary School
Avon, OH

Sharon I. Byrdsong
Senior Director of Alternative Options
Norfolk Public Schools
Norfolk, VA

Stephen D. Shepperd
Principal
Sunnyside Elementary School
Kellogg, ID

Dr. Otto Graf
Co-Director
Western Pennsylvania Principals Academy
University of Pittsburgh

About the Author

Paul G. Young, a retired elementary principal, is currently the Executive Director of the West After School Center in Lancaster, Ohio. He began his career as a high school band director and then retrained to become a fourth-grade teacher before advancing to an elementary principalship in 1986.

He served as President of the Ohio Association of Elementary School Administrators (OAESA) in 1997 and was elected to the National Association of Elementary School Principals (NAESP) Board of Directors in 1998 (the only person elected by write-in ballot). He became President-Elect in 2001–2002 and served as the national president during the 2002–2003 school year. He retired in December 2004. Since then, he has served as an advocate for the advancement of equitable and affordable afterschool programming for all children.

Dr. Young completed a Bachelor of Fine Arts degree in music education in 1972 and a Master of Music degree in trombone performance in 1973, both at Ohio University (OU)–Athens. He earned a PhD in educational administration from OU in 1992. Young has taught undergraduate music classes at Ohio University–Lancaster for more than 25 years, and he continues to teach private trombone lessons. He is a strong advocate for the arts and is the past president of the Ohio University School of Music Society of Alumni and Friends.

His wife, Gertrude, also completed BFA and MM degrees from Ohio University. She is a vocal and instrumental music teacher in the Lancaster City Schools. Daughter Katie is the principal oboist with the Florida Orchestra in Tampa–St. Petersburg. She earned music education degrees and performance certificates from the Eastman School of Music and Rice University. Daughter Mary Ellen is a sales representative with McGraw-Hill Higher Education in Chicago. She is a graduate of the University of Cincinnati College of Business. She studied piano and French horn and continues to be an avid music lover.

Dr. Young is the author of *Mastering the Art of Mentoring Principals*; *You Have to Go to School, You're the Principal: 101 Tips to Make It Better for Your Students, Your Staff, and Yourself*; and *Mentoring Principals: Frameworks, Agendas, Tips, and Case Studies for Mentors and Mentees*, the last two of which are available from Corwin Press. He is a featured columnist with the "Administrator's Desk" for Education World (www.education-world .com/a_admin/). He has also written numerous articles about music, the arts, student management, afterschool programs, and the principalship for professional journals.

DEFINITION OF *STRUCTURE*

Mode of building, construction, or organization: arrangements of parts, elements, or constituents

A complex system considered from the point of view of the whole rather than of any single part

Anything composed of parts arranged together in some way; an organization

DEFINITION OF *DISCIPLINE*

Training to act in accordance with rules

Instruction (teaching) and exercise designed to train proper conduct or action

Punishment inflicted by way of correction and training

The training effect of experience, adversity, etc.

Subjection to rules of conduct or behavior, a state of order maintained by training and control

A set or system of rules and regulations

SOURCE: *American College Dictionary.* (1967). New York: Random House.

When a school is well structured and staff effectively manages student behavior . . .

- Office referrals are minimal
- Removals from school are infrequent
- Behavior incidents are minor and routine
- Success rate for individual behavior plans is high
- Staff/parent/administrative satisfaction is high

Introduction

It was mid-May, and I was completing my sixth year of service as principal of an elementary school located in one of the more desirable neighborhoods of our school district. The superintendent visited and announced that in August I would be transferred to the other side of the city, to a school located within the poorest voting precinct in the county. My self-esteem and confidence were shattered. After 23 years of successfully teaching high school band, fourth and fifth grades, and serving as an elementary principal, I felt like I was being demoted.

My predecessor had led for 15 years what was to become my fourth school to serve as principal. Upon this principal's retirement, the superintendent had decided that her successor should be a strong principal that could initiate change and improve the public image of the school. I was surprised that he selected me. I was comfortable in my school. Student performance was good. Parents were involved and seemed pleased with our results. Little did I know that the opportunity the superintendent was giving me would forever influence my leadership abilities and shape my career. I was to learn valuable lessons about the importance of gaining others' permission to lead (as explained in Maxwell, 2002) and how the little things make a big difference in turning around a school. The challenges of the new assignment forced me to analyze how simple, concrete concepts of school structure, if overlooked, detract from a staff's ability to achieve a cohesive and pleasant work and learning environment.

During the transition, I listened as the former principal shared stories about students' attitude and discipline. It seemed the frequency of student behavioral issues she experienced and dealt with were much greater than mine. I became increasingly concerned and dreaded the transfer.

As the new school year began, my realities proved to be everything my predecessor had described. My learning curve was extraordinarily steep. Much of what I'd read and studied about the challenges facing high-poverty, low-performing schools proved to be true. Students were loud, angry, and showed disrespect when teachers attempted to correct them.

Many parents encouraged their children to fight back as a way of solving their disagreements. Discipline referrals to my office were high. Teachers were frustrated and tired. Precious instructional time was lost resolving fights from the playground. I became exasperated with the constant struggle to reduce day-to-day behavioral issues.

I struggled to gain a clearer understanding of the school's low performance. The good news was that there were some master teachers within the staff. My secretary made the transfer with me and organized the office in a very efficient manner. The classified staff was among the best I'd ever worked with. Strong leadership was in place with the parent organization, and the existing volunteer program was among the best of any schools in the county. What accounted most for low achievement? As the months passed by, I began to see more clearly some of the causes.

While investigating specific playground fights, particularly among the boys, I discovered that many of their squabbles originated over control of a ball or simple violation of rules for their games. The kids played roughly. When they were in trouble and I questioned the whereabouts of the supervising teacher, a pattern began to emerge. Some teachers appeared to understand the importance of proximity and preventative intervention while supervising the playground, but others did not. I began to predict the number of office referrals based on which teacher was assigned to the playground duty.

I began losing my patience with those teachers who never seemed to capably supervise and manage the students. At times, the tone of my interactions with them, and the staff in general, was no better than in some of the teacher-student exchanges I'd observed in hallways after recesses. I was angry that problems persisted. My behavior was compromising relationships and endangering my ability to lead. During a staff meeting, as we were analyzing causes for playground problems, I remember my frustration boiled over into the statement, "Don't just stand there; blow your whistle!" I didn't realize it at the time, but I'd uttered such a concrete statement that all the staff finally understood my campaign for preventive rather than reactive supervision. That incident and statement helped shape the fundamental nature of subsequent decisions that led to a continuous-improvement change effort for our school.

At about that same time, during a training seminar sponsored by the Ohio Classroom Management Project, our small team heard a presenter explain the difference between discipline and punishment. Even though we assumed we each knew the meaning of the words, we experienced an "aha" moment. We realized that too many of our staff members regarded both terms as having negative connotations. When we began looking at discipline from a positive perspective, as teaching, we gained new insights and ideas about how changes could be further implemented at our school. It became clear that change would not occur until all the adults had concrete rather than abstract understanding of how students were to be supervised, how our operational procedures were to be structured, what each adult would have to know and be able to do, and how we could collectively work to prevent problems rather than react to them.

This story is shared so the reader can better understand my reason for writing this book. I was not the first principal, nor will I be the last, to be assigned to a challenging school—in a rural, small-city, suburban, or urban setting. Had I been an inexperienced, beginning principal, the problems I experienced might have escalated to a point of total chaos. I understand why some beginning teachers and principals become discouraged and quit. I've observed many aspiring principals who, once given a taste of the realities, rethink their career paths and choose alternatives to the principalship. My greatest joy would be to know that the advice within this book helped a struggling principal, a teacher, or an entire school staff overcome their frustrations. I survived and was able to lead change because of the wisdom shared by others. The results of my staff's efforts will be shared later.

The insights and advice shared in this book are intended to provide a commonsense, practical approach to analyzing and preventing weaknesses in school structure. As defined at the beginning of this book, structure involves "arranging the parts, elements, or constituents" of an organization. We analyzed our expectations and the levels of consistency when managing students in a variety of settings. Our focus was less on individual classroom management techniques or styles, and more on the understanding of expectations and construction of interactions and activities that led to an optimal learning and work environment for students and staff. Particularly, we brought clarity to those occurrences where students were most likely to lose group or self-control. We helped kids feel good about themselves and their learning. We made improvements in aesthetics, in and out of the building. We chose to be inclusive of all students. We redefined the vision and mission of our school and celebrated any positive changes or accomplishments that our students achieved. We adopted new expectations for classroom instruction, and we also focused on teaching students in other settings during the day and after school as well. We thoroughly planned before the school year began. We spent time in staff meetings revisiting our expectations, reflecting, and fine-tuning our road map to success.

Without acknowledgment of and attention to the small details of school structure, weaknesses and inconsistency can slowly erode any staff's ability to perform and ultimately maximize their students' potential to learn. The contents within this book are based on experience and lessons learned during 20 years as principal of four elementary schools, from networking experiences and interactions with hundreds of principals, and from the perspectives gathered while serving as a leader in both a state and national professional association for principals. David Duke (2004) suggests that staffs in low-performing schools must inventory their assets and clearly understand how the presence or the lack of certain factors can impact the turnaround of beleaguered schools. This book is designed to help readers identify and understand those factors, capitalize on their strengths, and enable discovery of others unique to their setting.

My staff undertook the challenge of creating an effective school operation by thoroughly reflecting on and analyzing our structures that were working and those that needed improvement. Change did not occur as a result of a one-shot professional development training. Instead, organizational topics were discussed frequently during inservice meetings, grade-level planning sessions, parent meetings, and Intervention Assistance Team meetings. The discussions focused on managing students and parents within the scope of schoolwide operations, not just classroom management. Slowly, our operations became noticeably more cohesive as teachers bought into simple, concrete concepts. They taught them, modeled them, and continuously reinforced them with students and parents. Gradually, discipline referrals diminished and teaching time increased. The school environment acquired a renewed sense of calm. There were days and weeks when students were seldom referred to the office. The public perception of the students' toughness dissipated. In May of 2002, before my sabbatical to serve as president of the National Association of Elementary School Principals (NAESP), West Elementary School's first-, fourth-, and sixth-grade students achieved the highest state proficiency reading scores in the district. We had arrived! I was never prouder of a teaching staff! Our focus on the little things had produced significant results in student learning and achievement—and satisfaction at our work.

It is my hope that your school staff will aspire to achieve similar results.

**Students who feel successful are
seldom behavioral problems.**

—Robert DiGiulio (2000)

PURPOSE OF THIS BOOK

This book was written to be a collection of ideas and advice that can serve as a reflective guide to help elementary school staffs identify many of the small, concrete, common factors related to school organization and people management that, if unattended over time, can erode climate, teacher productivity, and student achievement. The advice is intended to be merely that—each professional staff must reflect on and develop structures that produce desirable results in their own unique setting. This book should be used as a guide in the quest to isolate those small, concrete concepts and practices that are the foundation of every effective school operation. Furthermore, the contents highlight the important role that principals play in structuring their schools; establishing a vision and expectations; and clarifying performance norms for all staff members as well as students, parents, guardians, and volunteers. It contains practical tips and advice that can be replicated or adapted to improve the organization of any elementary school. A school's purpose and mission will be actualized, and learning results achieved, when all the adults come together and collectively identify what needs to be done to create a structured, high-functioning school.

The contents of this book can be used as discussion starters for staff inservices. They are also intended to generate other ideas; initiate roundtable discussions; support professional staff development; or provide benchmarks for reflecting on and developing structures, configurations, and efficacy in all school operations. Structure empowers the professional staff to work effectively with students and maximize time for instruction and learning.

This book is a compilation of the author's 35 years of personal observations, conversations, and wisdom shared by school leaders throughout the nation. The reader will also find references to research on student management, qualities of turnaround principals, and operational leadership by such experts as Boynton and Boynton (2005), DiGuilio (2000), Duke (2004), Glanz (2006), Sigford (2006), and others. The insights and analysis of organizational concepts within this book are intended to provide concrete, practical ideas and recommendations that affirm best practice. The book also offers the reader or a team of professionals a series of tips and descriptive ideas that can help shape the "What to do?" or "road map" strategies that must be developed for every individual school.

Where order within schools is a priority, there is evidence of good planning and observable adult behaviors that uniformly fulfill expectations. There is a preventative approach to problem solving. Data exists that displays a positive correlation between teaching students acceptable social skills and achieving desirable results. Kids understand limits. Experimentation and creativity flourish within predetermined bounds. The norms of effective group adult performance become the foundation that helps each teacher achieve competence with classroom management and student motivation.

The primary intended audiences for this book include all practicing principals and teachers. The advice and tips will also have broad, practical applicability for

- Preservice teachers and aspiring principals
- Staff development personnel
- College and university educators who train teachers and principals
- Paraprofessionals
- Resource personnel (social workers, counselors, psychologists, etc.)
- Classified personnel
- Substitutes
- Parent leaders
- Volunteers
- Superintendents
- Afterschool personnel
- Head Start and preschools
- Student leaders
- All individuals interested in notching up school effectiveness

Nothing should negate the importance of the fundamental elements of people management. Good structure facilitates effective organization of students and positive human interactions within every aspect of the school unit. Structure should be continuously reviewed and improved. New challenges require new solutions. For success, all staff members must help envision and create new structures, clearly understand them, and buy into the little things and procedures that will make them work.

Excellence is to do a common thing in an uncommon way.

—Booker T. Washington

OVERVIEW OF THE CONTENTS

When reflecting on ways to develop a comprehensive school structure, it seems logical to break a typical day or year into parts in chronological arrangement. That is how the contents of this book are organized. Chapter 1 deals with beginnings—the aspects of structure that must be analyzed and implemented to assure a smooth start to the school year and each day. Chapter 2 focuses on structural components that impact instruction. Chapter 3 includes organizational tips and advice that should be considered midway through the year or day. Chapter 4 encompasses structures that overarch the year and day. Chapter 5 deals with reflections and considerations that draw endings and conclusions. Starting with the time children arrive on school property until they are dismissed to the care of their parents, the book includes a series of time-tested thoughts and discussions about structural issues that impact student and adult learning, performance, cohesiveness, and effectiveness in the five distinct parts of a day or year outlined in this book. Within the chapters, many of the tips and vignettes can stand alone as topics for staff development and reflection. Collectively, and with the reader's own insights for varied environments, they support the foundation of sound school structure. The insights and advice are intended to help guide professional staffs in their understanding of how small efforts add up and can prevent and eliminate bigger problems.

A recurring theme within each chapter is the focus and attention on moments of time and student supervision where staff performance can become inconsistent. All professional staffs will benefit from regular opportunities to reflect on and identify the times of day where expectations are unclear and where adults sometimes let down their guard while supervising students.

Despite our schools' unique differences (large/small, wealthy/poor, rural/urban, diverse/homogeneous), there are many commonalities. Readers are encouraged to reflect on the suggestions provided and engage others in discussions about additional organizational structures that will enhance student learning opportunities in their school. Using the inventory tools at the end of each chapter and based on individual or collective assessments of school organization, it is hoped that readers will be motivated to take action, provide solutions to problems they might be experiencing, adapt and apply ideas from this book to their setting and environment, and realize the benefits that improved structure has upon effectiveness and levels of productivity.

If you work with people who are difficult, there is both good news and bad news. The bad news is you work with them. The good news is you have time to study them, understand the patterns of their behavior, and plan your strategic response.

—Rick Brinkman and Rick Kirschner (2006)

**People like structure because it provides
information on how things should be done.**

—Annette L. Breaux and Harry K. Wong (2003)

Everyone is a leader, because everyone influences someone.

—John C. Maxwell (2002)

Beginnings: The Day and the Year

Ideas and Advice That Support and Facilitate Smooth Starts, Safe Arrivals, Efficacy of Time, and Effective Supervision of Students

If you stumble out of the starting blocks, you'll likely have a poor showing at the finish line.

—Paul Young

INTRODUCTION

On a typical morning during any school term, students arrive at elementary schools of all types—public, private, or independent—ready to learn. How they spend time, indoors or out, waiting for classes to begin; how they are greeted and supervised; how parents are received; and how students enter the school and proceed to their classrooms all contribute to a positive or negative experience. A bad start can ruin a child's day or year and no doubt that of numerous adults.

This chapter focuses on issues of student and adult safety, security, well-being, and efficient school operation. In addition, organizational concepts related to developing a vision and mission, planning, reflecting, using time wisely, supervising and assuring the welfare of students, and engaging parents are intertwined through several subsections. The scenarios and vignettes are presented in plain, direct language in an attempt to vividly illustrate how analysis of these factors can create effective schoolwide structure resulting in positive behaviors. Readers are encouraged to reflect and to determine other concepts and interrelated considerations that, when applied to their school's unique configuration, size, setting, and environment, can bolster school structure and efficient operation. At the end of the chapter, a checklist is provided to guide an individual reader's or a study group's reflection and analysis of organizational structures as each is applied to an identified school. Reflection, analysis of strengths and weaknesses, problem solving, and clarification of the organizational components presented in this chapter, and those unique to other schools, will increase staff and parent satisfaction, operational effectiveness, and productivity.

Before the beginning of the school year, take time to consider some fundamental structures of your school—structures such as your school's mission and its vision statement. McDonald's employees, from executives to line servers, know that their business is to sell tasty, fast food cheaply with efficient, reliable service. That sums up why they exist and how they hope to do business. Does your school mission and vision statement provide such clear focus? Can all school employees recall it? Is it child focused? Is your mission and vision statement philosophical, wordy, complicated, and hard to understand? Before tackling any other aspects of school structure, clarify and develop a short, succinct mission and vision statement. The best mission and vision statements clearly establish the purpose of the school (reason for being) and provide insight into core beliefs and norms of behavior. They are most effective when parents and students understand the benefits and outcomes of their involvement.

Next, confirm that your school's handbooks are up-to-date: student, parent, staff, volunteers, substitute, and so forth. These should be reviewed at least once each year. They are the guides from which many administrative decisions must be made. They should provide answers to students' and parents' most frequently asked questions. Information should be included that explains the following:

- General considerations for student safety and welfare while at school, particularly on the playground
- Emergency drills and evacuation procedures, including school lockdown drills
- Disciplinary procedures, due process, and conflict resolution
- School district policies on harassment and discrimination
- School district policies on dangerous weapons

- Standards for student grooming, behavior, and responsibility
- Procedures for handling student illness, absence, and distribution of medications
- Homework policies, procedures, and expectations
- Student enrollment, arrival, departure, release, and withdrawal procedures
- Parent involvement, visitations, and volunteer opportunities

Finally, there are numerous other considerations that support school structure. To name just a few, you might investigate school uniforms, a code of ethics, homework help lines, automated calling systems, or "Friday Food Grab Bags" for students unlikely to have sufficient food until the following Monday. The list can go on and on. You'll find many of these addressed in the remaining chapters. The point is to reflect, inventory, and affirm what you do well, and plan and discuss what will make your school structure more effective and produce greater results. Then, do something about the problems that are identified and the ideas that are generated. Make it a regular practice that after a period of time, the staff studies the data and results of your school's practices. Based on that analysis, some plans may need to be tweaked, others suspended, and the most effective established as site norms.

"That's All I Want for My Child"

Ricardo, the principal, was concerned that efforts to rewrite the school's mission statement had been so difficult. The results of several brainstorming and discussion sessions were less than he'd hoped for. So he added the topic to the summer planning retreat. It was near the end of that work session that consensus began to emerge.

Consuelo, an invited parent representative, had listened intently to the teachers' lengthy discussion of the school's lofty goals. She observed discussions go back and forth as individuals made suggestions about vision, purpose, and expectations, that were only to be challenged and discarded when other points of view were presented. There were several positive, but wordy mission statements written on chart paper. She tried to understand and internalize them all, but with difficulty. As she listened, she contemplated how each statement "fit" her son, José.

José had been diagnosed with Down syndrome and had many special needs. But he was learning and satisfactorily included in many

(Continued)

(Continued)

classes with children his age. Gaining her confidence to speak, Consuelo's words quickly brought clarity to the school's mission and vision—a process that had taken months to this point.

"I appreciate the professional insights and the efforts of this wonderful staff to create a mission statement that will guide this school. As I listen to your discussion, I think of my son, José. Most of you know about him and his needs. I know the statements you are writing are important and contain ideas and goals you all want to see occur for children at this school. But I just want three things for José."

Realizing that all eyes and attention were focused upon her, she continued, "First, I want José to graduate with the basic skills he will need to get a job that will challenge him to his fullest potential." Everyone nodded and agreed that the statement was appropriate for all children. Continuing, Consuelo said, "Second, I want José to acquire good social skills so that if he buys the house next door, none of you or anyone else in this community would want to move. And the third thing I want for my son is for him to grow up and appreciate the finer things of life—music, art, sports, cultural differences—and have skills that will enable him to spend his leisure time effectively. That's all I want for my child."

Immediately, everyone began to agree that the three statements pretty well summarized all any parent would want. The goals were the same as they desired for their children. Within minutes, they further condensed the three points and agreed upon the following:

The Mission of ABC School Community is to enable lifelong learners to master skills for the work and play place, for society, and for their individual pursuit of happiness.

The new mission and subsequent vision statements helped Ricardo guide the staff and school community in the months and years that followed. When new ideas were suggested, they were first analyzed to determine if they aligned with the mission. If they did not, they were not tried. When the ideas did complement the mission, they further contributed to the school's focus, goals, and student productivity.

1.1—PLAN FOR EFFECTIVE MORNING PLAYGROUND SUPERVISION

Playground supervision should never be taken lightly. It should always be a topic of every staff's continuous improvement planning.

Depending on where you live and work, the weather can vary and possibly reach extremes. Weather-related issues can become stressful and an inconvenience unless you learn to accept change in a positive way. Weather extremes can potentially create numerous challenges for teachers, para-professionals, and principals that share responsibility for playground supervision. The leadership style of the principal sets the tone for every-thing at the school and can empower or stagnate the best ideas and efforts of staff. For example, if the principal prepares for and takes weather-related issues in stride, so will the staff, students, and parents. Plan ahead for all probable conditions—extreme cold and heat, rain, winds, thunderstorms, tornados, earthquakes, and threats from intruders.

WHAT TO DO?

- Determine the environmental conditions under which students will be allowed on the playground.
- Assure that all staff members understand how and by whom those decisions are made.
- Model expectations of playground behavior and be attentive to potential dangers. Adults should have unobstructed visual coverage of all parts of the playground. They should also assure that all visitors, parents, or volunteers have obtained authorization to be on the playground. Any intruders or suspicious activities in the vicinity of the playground should be reported to proper authorities.
- Assure that plans have been reviewed by local authorities and school district officials and that they have been communicated to parents.

Plan for effective playground supervision. Spend adequate time with the entire staff discussing expectations for both students and adults. Assure that all adults responsible for playground supervision understand their responsibilities. Then, *Do* the plan for a designated amount of time. At a designated point in the year, *Study* the results, then *Act* on recommended and agreed-upon changes (Plan, Do, Study, Act—PDSA). Plan for the inside supervision of children when it rains. When it is extremely cold, develop a plan and designate space to supervise the children who will inevitably be dropped off before the designated time. Your plan will never pass public relations standards if children are refused entry and left outside in the cold. Each school campus has unique parameters, characteristics, and challenges that must be addressed by your staff.

Whenever possible, children need time to run and play and to interact regularly in socially acceptable ways with each other and adults. Don't shortchange children's playtime. Considering that the number of overweight children (and adults) is steadily increasing, take advantage of every minute to engage students (and yourself) in physical activity. Are students allowed to run and play prior to the entrance bell? Must they be closely managed to control fights? Do they run free (and perhaps wild?) or are rules and guidelines enforced that create order and safety? Focus on creating structures during morning playtime that allow opportunities for strenuous activity. Numerous studies show than an increase in students' stamina can lead to higher achievement levels in the classroom.

Without the establishment of limits and expectations, expect chaos. Create a kid-friendly playground, but maintain adult control. That is, engage with students while they are playing. Students love it when adults talk with them, play games, walk and run, and smile. Remember, the adults are role models for the playground.

1.2—ALLOW RECESS IN THE MORNING

Public health officials and news reporters are collaborating to elevate the topic of childhood obesity and the risks and dangers for children that have limited recess time or other opportunities for rigorous activities through-out the day. Even though there may be valid reasons for limiting some games or recess time—uncontrollable behaviors, lack of space, pressure to bring up test scores, unsafe conditions—concerned staffs attuned to cur-rent fitness and nutrition information should find numerous ways to get lethargic kids moving before it is mandated from elsewhere.

Pushed by the need to improve test results, many principals and their staffs have removed morning recess times from their schedules. However, what may seem like a good idea now might later create more serious prob-lems for kids as adults. Researchers predict that the current generation of young children, without better nutrition and increased levels of exercise, may experience a life span that is shorter than that of their parents (Dietz, 1998). The fitness habits formed during childhood often remain the same for a lifetime.

A reality, also, is that many decisions that shortchange recess time, made under the pretext to increase instructional time, are influenced by other unspoken motivators that must be addressed by every staff. Some of these include the following:

- Many teachers do not like to supervise recess.
- Many adults fail to acknowledge the benefits of exercise.
- Too much instructional time is lost making lines, getting kids in order, moving from place to place—not the kids' fault but rather the supervising adults who lack a sense of organization and time.

- Teachers assume kids can't refocus quickly after recess, therefore they don't expect it.
- Negotiated contracts dictate conditions for the benefit of adults at the expense of students.

An effective staff will continuously reevaluate their school's practices, procedures, and structures. They will organize themselves in ways that reduce periods of wasted time, focus on desired results, and do what is best in the long run for kids.

> **What we stop doing is sometimes the most important thing we can do.**
>
> —Noah benShea

1.3—FORM AND TRAIN A SAFETY PATROL

In many locations, the student safety patrol is a long-standing, community-supported practice and service-learning opportunity for students. However, the thought of crossing busy streets can elevate the stress levels of young children—as well as teachers and principals. To help, it makes good sense to position reliable older students, adult volunteers, or staff at busy intersections and crosswalks. All too often, however, once those arrangements have been made, no one of authority from the school ever checks to make sure the intended results are being achieved.

WHAT TO DO?

- Assign a staff member to train and monitor the students as they perform their duties.
- Enlist the support of volunteers who live near busy intersections. Their physical presence can support students and help prevent problems.
- Engage the support of the police and other local authorities in developing and supporting safety patrols. They can assist with training and supporting students' service-learning opportunities.
- Write grants and secure funding sources that support the creation of safe walking routes to school (see www.saferoutesinfo.org).

Trained, conscientious safety patrol members create positive public relations and become good school ambassadors. Their training and experience support good citizenship and personal responsibility. When asked, various businesses and service groups will often provide resources for support of the safety patrol.

All staff members should demonstrate concern and care for the students serving as part of the safety patrol. Responsibility for scheduling, training, and organizing the students each day might be delegated to a few, but everyone should be aware of the expectations. They should encourage the students selected for the patrol and assure that their actions contribute to *all* students' safety.

1.4—TEACH EXPECTATIONS TO STUDENTS WHILE LINING UP AFTER THE BELL SOUNDS

It never seems to fail that children will antagonize each other, physically or verbally, when forming a line. It's no wonder that certain adults sometimes continue to do the same. Effective playground supervisors know that their proximity to children will prevent most interpersonal conflicts from ever developing. When children abuse each other in front of adults, the dispute has likely been festering for some time, or they lack respect for the adults or have no fear of consequences. The latter should be more of a concern for principals than the former.

WHAT TO DO?
• Adopt a proactive and preventive approach to solving problems when forming student lines. Positive considerations work much better than always reacting to what students have done.
• When performing supervisory duties, teachers should position themselves so that they can always be seen and heard by the children.
• Paint or mark a designated line on the ground where each homeroom class should congregate and form a line. If desired, structure and space a consistent length to the line.
• Assign challenged students a designated position within the line that is close to where the supervising adult will be.
• Teach students how to maintain personal space between each other.
• Teach students when it is appropriate to talk and when it is not.

All staff members must collectively envision the standards of acceptable supervisory performance and consistently adhere to them. Likewise, they should practice with students until appropriate behaviors standards are observable each day. Vary your procedures, students' order in line, and any other aspects of queuing lines that might become stale over time. Never stop teaching and reinforcing expectations. Set a positive, welcoming tone. Treat children with respect, and they will do the same.

1.5—BUILD RELATIONSHIPS WITH PARENTS

There never seems to be enough time each morning to prepare for the day's lessons. In many schools, teachers are planning, grading papers, preparing materials, reviewing data, waiting to make copies, or simply catching up on the weekend's events. Most of that work is necessary for a successful day; some of it is not.

Every school should have numerous, noticeable indicators that parents are welcome at school. These indicators should include pleasant name recognition from all staff, not just the secretary.

WHAT TO DO?

- Place welcoming signs at main entrances.
- Develop a procedure for greeting parents and meeting their needs in an efficient manner.
- Create a reception area with coffee and tea.
- Create a parent resource room.
- Review your school's Web site. Is it parent friendly? Does it provide current information that successfully markets your school? Is it a source of school pride?

Each school staff should include a committee that focuses on parent reception and involvement. This committee should continuously assess school practices and services. Committee members should review the success of parent-welcoming strategies by surveying new parents.

Many elementary school staffs have earned parents' trust and respect for their initiatives to create a welcoming environment. They likely hold family nights, morning coffee clubs, luncheons, and career days, and employ key personnel to meet parents' diverse needs. However, the most successful, longest-lasting results are achieved and sustained when each staff member routinely and genuinely greets each parent with respect, conveys concern for all children, encourages a partnership, and wears a warm smile.

Another recommendation for a successful day is to greet and interact with parents in the gathering area. It takes only a few minutes, and being available to interact, listen, and develop positive relationships—if even for a brief time—can have big payoffs. Teachers might also venture forward and greet parents in the parking lot. Welcome them, open the doors for their children, exchange warm greetings, and wish them a good day. Assure them that you will have a great day with their child. Parents can observe "the teacher" and put a name with a face. They will see that you are concerned about children and approachable. Over time, many will begin to think you walk on water!

Many teachers extend positive overtures to parents on the first few days of school but soon fall into less hospitable habits and a busy routine. When a staff comes together and sustains efforts to greet parents each day, public relations, communication, support, and involvement increase. Parents advocate for the school as one of choice where open enrollment is allowed.

A school system without parents at its foundation is just like a bucket with a hole in it.

—Rev. Jesse L. Jackson

Which Would You Choose?

If you were a child, which of these lines would you have hoped to be in?

Teacher A's third graders were dismissed from the school's morning gathering area to their classroom by the playground supervising teacher. When the children arrived at the classroom door, Teacher A, seated at her desk, looked up and motioned the line leader through the door. Teacher A was pleasant but didn't get up from her desk while the children went about unpacking book bags and doing other typical morning routines. A paraprofessional moved about the room helping children with special needs, collecting parent notes, taking attendance, and organizing homework papers.

Teacher B, who greeted her class at the gathering area, turned the task of quickly moving 25 children to her third-floor classroom into a fun game, effectively supervising all of them at the same time.

At the classroom door, she greeted each child individually with a question and they accurately responded with a math fact, a state capital city, or a fact about current events. The kids never knew what kind of question she'd greet them with, but they excitedly thought they couldn't get into her room if they didn't get it right. Knowing her children's ability, Teacher B helped each get off to a positive start. Once inside, she orchestrated every detail of the morning routine with precision. Collecting parent notes didn't require as much time because she'd already collected many from kids she'd seen on the playground. Teacher B never sat down except to gather the children for story time. She rarely used her desk. She never wasted time. Her students met her expectations and excelled.

Not surprisingly, parents will overwhelmingly choose Teacher B. They can readily observe the contrasts in effectiveness between practices. And they will talk among themselves about what they observed, what they prefer for their children, and other perceptions of the school and its staff in the parking lot on their way to work. It should be no surprise how teachers earn their good, and bad, reputations. The most conscientious parents will do whatever they can to have their child assigned to Teacher B. Read more about how a professional staff might handle issues related to that topic in Chapter 5.

1.6—TEACH CHILDREN TO MOVE QUIETLY THROUGH THE HALLWAYS

Getting children from one place in the school to another without being loud and disruptive to others can be a constant challenge. Some teachers can supervise this task effectively, while those who are lax permit their children to talk, pick at each other and items displayed on walls, or engage in behaviors that eventually require intervention and time away from teaching and learning. Attention to small details will result in much less teacher stress and fewer discipline problems. The principal is more likely to observe and assess teachers' management of students in the hallways than in classrooms.

So what are the secrets of master teachers when moving lines of children through the hallways?

- They envision the results they want and expect to see.
- They have observed other master teachers perform this task many times.

- They direct and teach children the appropriate behaviors they expect during the task.
- They practice with their children.
- They continuously monitor with eyes and ears.
- They never allow a line to spread further than they can see or hear.
- They acknowledge the importance of managing this task as it relates to their overall effectiveness as a teacher.

An Unexpected Lesson From the Field

Compared with other schools, there was a noticeably higher noise level inside Maple Street School. Steve, the principal, was concerned. He'd tried to motivate his veteran staff to "tighten the screws" when supervising students in the hallways. But nothing changed. Veteran teachers said the building was louder than others where they'd worked because of acoustics.

Then one October day, while conducting walk-throughs of classrooms, Steve noticed an increase in noise level of children's voices around a corner in the direction of the library. Curious as to what might be happening and who the group of children was that was making the noise, Steve began walking to investigate.

Then he heard Carlos, a first-year teacher, say, "Spot Check!" and the noise abruptly ceased. When Steve rounded the corner, he saw Carlos observing his 25 second graders—aligned, motionless, and *quiet*! The immediate impact on the hallway noise was dramatic.

Later, Steve asked Carlos to further explain his management strategy. Carlos reviewed the list of expectations and the manners he had taught his students, such as how to stay within their own personal space, refrain from talking, and pay attention to the whereabouts of the teacher at all times. He said the kids loved the game of freezing in space when he said, "Spot Check." They never knew when he might ask it, but like bootcamp inductees, they competed with each other, hoping never to be the last to be caught "freezing." They also knew there were class rewards if they worked together so that Carlos never had to say, "Spot Check." Carlos further explained that the longer they had played "Spot Check," the less he needed it to reduce noise, but he kept doing it occasionally because the kids enjoyed it so much.

Steve immediately recognized a master teacher in the rough. He asked Carlos to describe the practice at a staff meeting. Carlos agreed, although anxious about how he might be perceived as a beginning teacher showing veterans what to do.

> Steve used the opportunity, not to institute "Spot Check" for all classrooms, but to reflect on the increasing noise levels of the school and strategies to reduce it. He realized he should have tackled the issue much earlier. He clarified his expectations, and he challenged all staff to better supervise and to experiment with creative management strategies.
>
> By Thanksgiving, the hallways were noticeably quieter. By spring vacation, other principals were visiting Maple Street School to observe strategies they could use in their schools.

1.7—LOCK THE DOORS

Once the students are inside the building, secure it by locking the doors. Post signs indicating the state code that limits outside access except at the main entrance. Inform all staff and parents of the security policy and its rationale. Then question your reliable vendors and visitors about the number of building doors through which they have been able to gain unauthorized access. You might be surprised by the frequency that professionally dressed men and women are allowed entry because "you look like you have business here."

It may be inconvenient for parents and visitors, even school board members, to walk to the main entrance. Issue keys to those who need them, but also stand strong under potential criticism. Lock the doors to protect children from outside intruders. It just makes good sense.

1.8—STRUCTURE HOMEROOM ACTIVITIES

Typically, effective teachers are observed engaging their students in learning activities as soon as children enter the classroom door. In contrast, for some, precious instructional minutes are lost while they are "getting it together."

While the morning announcements are being made, the teacher should model good listening skills and record necessary information on the blackboard or delegate this task to someone. However, while that is taking place, numerous other tasks can be accomplished: attendance, lunch counts, homework collection, and so forth. Effective practices are too numerous to list here, but every student teacher and beginner should seek out master teachers for their best ideas and advice.

WHAT TO DO?

The point is this—don't waste time.

Teach the homeroom morning details and routines so that the children will carry on and do them even when a substitute is present. Include a brief period of time for whole-group learning of calendar activities and other cognitive activities (discussion of current events or other developmentally appropriate learning skills or tasks) that help children focus and warm up their brains. Periodically conduct a class meeting and allow children to share personal facts about themselves and their families. To best utilize time and avoid embarrassing situations, establish limits on what are appropriate topics and identify those that are not.

Serious athletes or musicians wouldn't think to engage in their activity until they have stretched their muscles or warmed up. Morning homeroom activities are the calisthenics for learning.

1.9—PROVIDE UNIVERSAL BREAKFAST IN THE CLASSROOM

There are still some educational leaders and teaching staffs that feel it is not the school's responsibility to provide breakfast for children. Likely, they have ethical or moral attitudes that shape their thinking and feel that parents have sole responsibility for providing breakfast. However, when hungry children lose their ability to concentrate, or act out, or engage in antisocial behaviors, those same educators often assume kids have no interest in learning. Research from the U.S. Department of Agriculture (2006) clearly supports the benefits of beginning each day with breakfast. In 2004, nearly 9 million children participated in school breakfast programs in the United States.

The reasons kids come to school without breakfast are too numerous to list. For many, poverty is not the cause. Whatever the reasons might be, too many kids are hungry. School officials are unlikely to change students' or parents' morning habits and assure that *all* kids eat at home. However, it is within their realm of influence to provide universal breakfast at school—and in each classroom.

Many complaints about serving breakfast are masked behind adults' unwillingness to do the work necessary to provide it. In schools with high need, serving breakfast to everyone takes time and space. Despite our best efforts, some students still miss the serving opportunities—or are embarrassed to have their friends know they are hungry.

> ## WHAT TO DO?
>
> Check with your school district food service administrator to deter-
> mine eligibility as well as state and federal rules and guidelines for pro-
> viding breakfast programs in your area. The food service and business
> administrators should have current information about funding sources.
> Providing universal breakfast in the classroom can take less time than
> you think, can involve lower personnel costs, and can even create a
> profit for the food service department because of increased participa-
> tion rates, and it assures access for all students.
>
> Despite what some might think, teachers can manage more than
> one activity at a time. So can the kids. Adults simply have to be willing
> to try. Success hinges on a staff's willingness to recognize a need,
> restructure the day, and act positively with the best interests of
> children foremost on their minds.
>
> In schools where breakfast is served in classrooms, referrals to the
> nurse or office for headaches, lack of attention, and inappropriate
> behavior are noticeably reduced. Tardiness is less frequent, and academic
> gains increase (Kennedy & Cooney, 2001).

1.10—MAKE MORNING ANNOUNCEMENTS

Structure is missing in schools where principals make announcements
"when they get around to it" or not at all. If all teachers began instruction
"when they got around to it" or they felt like it, student achievement
would suffer. Expectations drop, organization and planning falter, and
interruptions become more frequent.

> ## WHAT TO DO?
>
> Immediately after the last morning bell rings, the principal (or designee)
> should start morning announcements over the public address system.
> Encourage students to assist. They can help announce the lunch menu,
> guest teachers, and other information of interest to staff, students, vol-
> unteers, and visitors. Conclude with the Pledge of Allegiance and sing a
> patriotic song. If many languages are spoken in your area, learn words
> and phrases and say them publicly. Expose children to other languages
> and cultures even if everyone speaks the same language. Recognize an

(Continued)

(Continued)

individual or small group (sometimes an entire class) for displaying good citizenship and adhering to the code of conduct by allowing them to lead the pledge and song. Encourage parents to visit and videotape this special occasion for their child. It starts each day in a positive way.

The principal should take two or three minutes to reflect, teach, and clarify routine expectations about behavior, learning goals, and common courtesies for students and adults. This can be the time to set the tone for the school. It is important that people hear the leader's voice and that a positive focus on learning and behavior is established each day.

Morning announcement time can be accomplished in less than five minutes. To avoid dullness, the routine may require minor changes to keep it fresh. But most kids (and adults) will benefit from the consistency of structure.

The principal's announcements set a positive tone. As the day goes forward, nothing less should be expected from the staff.

How Fast Can Students Go?

At the back-to-school staff meeting, Rochelle, a new principal, was clarifying expectations for how she envisioned time to be spent during morning homeroom activities. She explained that she would begin making public address announcements promptly after the 9:00 tardy bell. She stated that the announcements would include information for both students and adults, a student-led reading of the daily lunch menu, and a listing of birthdays and coming events. She would review and comment on building expectations, provide commendations, and recognize students caught being good. A schoolwide recitation of the Pledge of Allegiance and singing of a patriotic song would conclude the daily routine.

While talking to the staff, she noticed increasing looks between people and sidebar conversations beginning while she further explained what she expected to be accomplished during the announcement period. She unveiled her vision, which included students and teachers listening, reviewing, and recording important information; collecting homework and parent notes; distributing breakfast; recording attendance and the lunch count via the computer; and transitioning into homeroom learning activities. She expected all this to be accomplished in less than 15 minutes.

As she was about to move forward with the next agenda topic, Sally Mae erupted into tears, exclaiming, "My kindergarten students can't move that fast!" Rochelle feared losing control of the meeting as other teachers began to agree with Sally Mae. Comments such as "This will never work" and "Why do we have to do all this so fast?" echoed throughout the room. "How do you expect me to open the breakfast milk cartons for all my students?" Sally Mae cried. "You come show me how I am supposed to get all this done!"

Taken aback, Rochelle grasped for a response that wouldn't embarrass Sally Mae. But before she could, Sarah, a primary-grade special education teacher, volunteered to assist Sally Mae and her students. "I can help your kids," she told her. "I'll have a student who should be included in your classroom at that time. I can help, and I know we can get everything done."

Rochelle was sure this wouldn't be the end of the matter. But to her surprise, the issue was never raised again. Sarah not only helped Sally Mae with morning announcement time, her example of determination and efficacy also helped Sally Mae develop new strategies and a different perspective on expectations. These became a source of renewed inspiration and energy that, for years, Sally Mae had been missing.

The positive example from the kindergarten room spread. Teachers began reflecting and identifying periods of time throughout the day that could be redirected to save instructional time. Time spent putting on students' coats and boots, getting drinks at the water fountain, and washing hands was reduced—simply by better directing the activities and encouraging the students. With a new outlook, teachers reevaluated what young students could do for themselves and what actually required adult assistance.

How fast could they go? Certainly more quickly than was commonplace before Rochelle arrived. The higher the expectations, the more teachers learned how their students could meet them. Their school became a more exciting, productive place to work and learn.

1.11—CHECK BOOK BAGS AND HOMEWORK PLANNERS

Quietly, while the morning announcements take place or shortly thereafter, teachers and paraprofessionals should encourage students to empty their book bags and place assignments in designated areas. Homework planners should be opened to the current date and attention drawn toward any notes from parents. Keep a file of all parent notes for later reference and documentation. Staff should closely follow this daily routine. Missing a critical message from a parent can escalate strained home–school relations and communication.

Children can help with this simple procedure by organizing their desk area, placing materials in clear view of the teacher, and copying special information in their planners that the teacher has written and posted for all to see. They can check off assignments that have been completed and organize papers to be taken home. Don't underestimate their abilities. Teaching expectations, reinforcing them, monitoring the room as an activity takes place, and praising positive outcomes will produce desired outcomes.

1.12—DO THE SHIRTS AND THE PANTS TOUCH?

If your school has a dress code, enforce it. If there isn't one, consider writing one. Many schools and districts adopt uniform policies. Dress codes must meet legal standards as well as conform with students' constitutional rights. The courts also uphold the right and responsibility of administrators to maintain order and safety within the scope of the school day and year. Attire that creates disruption can be prohibited. This topic should be addressed in student-parent handbooks and back-to-school assemblies.

Most visitors will tell you that order and discipline are better in schools with a dress code. In the upper grades where students' hormones begin raging and the limits are tested more frequently, a dress code is your guide to establishing those boundaries.

Establish a "no hat" rule in your school. Removing hats inside public buildings used to be a common rule of etiquette. When adults visit, there are ways that they can be politely asked to remove their hats while at school. Print the rules of etiquette in handbooks, at entry locations, in newsletters and concert programs, and elsewhere for the public's information. Clarify the expectations and their justification in a positive manner. Most people will applaud your efforts.

1.13—NO TALKING DURING EMERGENCY DRILLS

To establish an orderly and safe evacuation of a school, students must be taught not to talk. Some might become excited, others frightened, but all students can learn to leave the building silently while listening to calm directions of adults. Practice this with them. Repeat drills when they don't meet expectations. Adults must convey the seriousness of the situation. In the event of an actual emergency, students trained to remain composed and quiet will listen and respond to adults they respect without panicking.

During these drills, the principal and custodian should randomly block exits. Teach students and adults to quickly respond and react to any situation. From time to time, the principal should hide a student or volunteer to assure that proper attendance is taken and all inhabitants of the school are accounted for. Plan an evacuation drill during lunch. Emergencies can occur anytime and anywhere, including during the lunch periods.

Have a plan to relocate all students and staff to one or more alternative, safe locations within walking distance. Communicate the plans to all adults. Take necessary important records, rosters, and emergency and parent phone numbers with you. Predetermine a leader and spokesperson in the event the principal cannot evacuate the building. Utilize cell phones, but have a backup communication plan if all power sources are disrupted. Have cash and a credit card in the event the emergency evacuation is real.

Be prepared, practice, and insist on order and quiet. Expect nothing less than total compliance from students and adults.

1.14—ESTABLISH A STUDENT COUNCIL

Allow students an opportunity to voice their opinions and contribute to the structure of *their* school. Student councils, when effectively organized, can contribute a vital service to the school's mission. Some tips for ensuring their success include the following:

- Select good advisors. It is best if those individuals are staff members. Parents have also enjoyed success as advisors. In some schools, cooks and custodians have played a key role within student governance.
- Teach children how to conduct an effective meeting using basic rules of parliamentary procedure.
- Teach and prepare students to speak publicly and coach them to improve their skills.

- Encourage the student council to initiate projects and accept responsibilities beyond simply organizing special spirit days or fundraising.
- Operate from a set of by-laws.
- Connect the student council with others in nearby schools as well as with state and national professional associations.
- Assure staff support and buy-in.
- As the principal, it is vital that you acknowledge and demonstrate strong support for the student council.
- Allow student council representatives to conduct building tours for visitors. Students have a perspective of the school that should be acknowledged. Your guests will likely tell you it was the best tour they ever experienced!

> Visit the Web site of the National Association of Elementary School Principals (NAESP) for information and numerous resources that support student councils. The wealth of incentives, recognitions, and professional materials you will find will help you achieve your goals and lead your school to success (see www.naesp.org/nprc).

1.15—ESTABLISH STUDENT INCENTIVES AND RECOGNITIONS

Most people are driven by incentives. Pride and recognition are powerful motivators. The school year needs to be structured to allow time for public recognitions and celebration of success. Words of recognition and individual acknowledgment of effort will go a long way in developing a child's sense of pride and worth. Make sure your school has numerous venues and positive practices for acknowledging good work—for both students and adults.

1.16—EMPOWER STAFF TO DEVELOP SCHEDULES

The creation of the weekly schedule of music, art, physical education, and related classes is a major responsibility for principals. Completion of that task in isolation will likely result in numerous errors, scheduling conflicts, and staff dissatisfaction. Add in complaints about the schedule of supervision for cafeteria and playground, and the collective criticism can divide a staff and alienate the principal.

Unless the negotiated agreement forbids otherwise, empower a committee of volunteer teachers to form the schedule. The principal should establish expectations and set the parameters. However, those that must work daily within the schedule better know the nuances that will work most effectively and will satisfy the most people. Developing schedules is a task where consensus of opinion is most desirable.

The principal should always maintain veto power and grant final approval. An experienced staff will find ways to expedite the work and address special needs of peers. There will be fewer complaints and a happier principal and staff!

1.17—LEARN ALL STUDENTS' NAMES

People love it when you can address them by their names, first as well as last. When they recognize that you also know something about them, it further validates their individuality and strengthens your relationship with them. Students will feel they have gained your acceptance and that they belong in "your" school. Work at remembering names by developing mind association games, looking for cues in classrooms, reviewing each child's grade card, spending time looking at class pictures and seating charts, mentally reviewing names while observing in classrooms, and saying some of the names over and over. Some students who act out frequently you'll know too well. Unfortunately, the well-behaved students—those who complete their work, follow the rules, and meet expectations—are those whose names people often fail to learn.

People appreciate the effort it requires to know their names. Visitors are always amazed by what they observe, especially in large schools, when staff members greet children by name and ask questions about a sibling or an activity associated with the child or family. Usually, the child beams. It makes his or her day.

It may be surprising, but young children sometimes don't know the last name of their friends—even their own family members. They may just know their grandmother as "Gigi." Everyone in the school will benefit from learning first and last names of the people they know.

Principals have great influence in their schools. Knowing names of people in the school community is a critical skill in developing that positive influence.

1.18—ESTABLISH AN EFFECTIVE INTERVENTION ASSISTANCE PROCESS

Intervention Assistance Teams (IATs) have a variety of names: Teacher Assistance Teams, Building Assistance Teams, staffings, and so forth. Whatever variation of the name you might know, there should be some commonalities in the ways these teams and the meetings they hold are organized and structured.

The IAT process first appeared in the literature in the 1970s and 1980s. Since that time, principals leading productive IATs have evolved the process to achieve greater results. Almost universally, without observable results in classrooms, teachers will quickly come to view the process as a hoop to jump through before a challenged student can be tested or placed in special classes. A climate where that motive is pervasive indicates a need to revisit the school's structure and develop a shared responsibility for success of all students.

The principal should establish the expectations of shared responsibilities of the intervention process at the start of the year. Teachers must collectively identify and acknowledge each other's curricular and pedagogical strengths. Then, when teachers begin noticing individual children falling behind in their classrooms, they can ask for support from colleagues by hanging a folder outside their classroom indicating a request for help. Inside the folder is a brief description of the student's problem, a seating chart, and picture of the challenged student. Any teacher walking past the hallway with a few minutes to spare can step inside the room, briefly observe, and record his or her ideas and suggestions. This voluntary practice, when well structured, generates teamwork and effective practices, and greatly reduces the need to move further in the intervention process.

However, there will be cases that require involvement of many others, an ongoing documentation of interventions, and a more structured process. At that point, a structured IAT process (see sample agenda, Figure 1.1) should be initiated using the following outline:

Step 1. The classroom teacher informally shares a child's ongoing problem with the principal, discusses attempted interventions, and requests advice and assistance.

Step 2. The principal suggests other interventions once the specific problem is clearly identified. Then, the teacher either agrees to try them or, perhaps based upon previous informal discussions or case priority, the principal refers the case to the IAT and schedules a meeting. The principal asks the teacher for recommendations of other "expert" staff or district personnel to invite or makes that decision later. The parent and child are invited to the meeting.

Step 3. The classroom teacher or other designee prepares the parent and child for the meeting and coaches each in preparing one new intervention they will offer and agree to implement following the meeting. The referring teacher must bring specific, varied sources of data to support the case rather than merely generalizations. The teacher must also come to the meeting with a new idea to offer.

Step 4. The meeting is scheduled and conducted for no longer than 25 minutes. Roles are assigned by the principal. The timekeeper assures that participants stay on task. IATs are best held before school when participants are fresh. A sample meeting agenda is included in Figure 1.1.

Step 5. During the meeting, participants stay focused on interventions and desired small successes rather than identifying and celebrating problems. The principal facilitates the meeting and prior to its end, assigns tasks, responsibilities, and timelines, and determines follow-up procedures.

Step 6. The process is repeated, if needed, when minimal success is obtained. The process is suspended if great strides are realized. An appropriate celebration can then be planned. With consensus and supportive data, referral for testing and special services can be made for identified cases.

Figure 1.1   Sample Agenda

IAT Meeting Agenda				
Time	**Task**	**Person/s Responsible**	**Action**	**Desired Outcome**
3 minutes	Introductions, review of process, assignment of meeting roles	Principal	Listening	Familiarity, breakdown of barriers
5 minutes	Clarification of problem	Referring teacher, parent, participants	Listening, asking probing questions	Focus on specific problem, avoid tackling broad range of related issues
5 minutes	Recommendation of interventions	All participants	Brainstorming	No evaluation or value placed on ideas
7 minutes	Selection of interventions	Referring teacher, parent, student	Discussion/ Selection	Intervention plan
5 minutes	Next steps, follow-up and meeting wrap-up	Principal	Assignment of tasks, responsibility and accountability for interventions, determination of timelines	Timeline, process for review, follow-up, and evaluation

Checklist for Assuring an
Effective School-Based Intervention Process

_____ At the beginning of the school year, as a staff professional development activity, teachers and principal collectively identify "experts" among the staff, those with recognized strengths and passion related to various aspects of reading, writing, math, science, time-on-task, motivation, etc. Everyone is identified with a minimum of one strength.

_____ Teachers focus attention during the first weeks of school on identifying and addressing all students' needs. Numerous interventions are tried and documented that address each individual student's specific behavioral, social, emotional, motivational, remedial, or acceleration needs.

_____ When specific interventions fail to achieve desired results, teachers hang folders outside their classrooms requesting a brief peer observation of a targeted student with recommendations. Any staff member with several free minutes voluntarily observes, offers support, or further documents the problem. A brief description of the problem (such as will be requested for further IAT involvement), a record of attempted interventions, a seating chart, a picture of the targeted student, and a paper for the peer supporter to record observations and recommendations are enclosed in the folder.

_____ If the problems persist, the teacher informally discusses the case with the principal.

_____ The principal suggests additional interventions and helps the teacher further identify and focus on the root cause of the problem. Together, they determine the time or process for the teacher to report on results of new interventions. The principal can delegate the case to other individuals only when they possess authority and influence to effect change. The case can be referred to the IAT if appropriate.

_____ Additional interventions are attempted. The teacher informally reports outcomes to the principal.

_____ After numerous failed intervention attempts by the teacher and others, the principal may decide to refer the case to the IAT. The principal asks the teacher for input as to "experts" to invite to the meeting and schedules it within two weeks.

_____ The secretary completes administrative paperwork and sends out invitations to the scheduled meeting. The student and parents or guardians are invited to the meeting.

_____ The teacher and other designated personnel coach and prepare the student and parents or guardians on their role and responsibilities prior to the meeting.

_____ A 25-minute Intervention Assistance Team meeting is held. Interventions are selected; timelines and documentation procedures are determined; and a follow-up meeting, if needed, is established. A focus is maintained on one or two problems and small, incremental, desirable steps toward change and progress.

_____ The process repeats if further intervention is necessary. The case can be referred for an independent or school evaluation if appropriate. The case is closed if interventions achieve desired results.

_____ All staff share responsibility for success for all students.

1.19—STRUCTURE EFFECTIVE MEETINGS

Nothing frustrates teachers more than a principal who comes late to a meeting. Even worse is to schedule and conduct a meeting and accomplish nothing. It really frustrates people when meetings bog down and extend past the scheduled time.

WHAT TO DO?

A good deal of each school staff member's time is spent in meetings. Leadership for meetings is best shared by all staff. To ensure that meetings produce results, prepare an agenda (see Figure 1.2) and distribute it in advance. Meetings will be most effective when those in charge of planning them consider the following:

- Provide written notice to those who are invited or expected to attend.
- Adhere to the starting and ending time.
- Establish group norms about prompt arrival, respect for others when brainstorming, sharing and critiquing ideas, and discussing sensitive topics.
- Delineate responsibilities for facilitating, reporting information, timekeeping, taking minutes, process evaluating, etc.
- Set discussion time limits and list expected outcomes.
- Determine in advance how and when decisions will need to be made.
- Develop follow-up plans when necessary.
- Evaluate meetings from time to time for effectiveness.

Much of designated staff members' time is spent, and sometimes wasted, participating in individualized education plan (IEP) meetings for children with specific and challenging learning needs. Ongoing, effective home–school communication can greatly reduce the time spent in these meetings. Only the meetings for students requiring many additional services should last more than an hour. Focus the discussion and don't allow people to waste valuable time or grandstand at IEP meetings.

Don't have meetings unless there is a good reason to have one. Meeting for the sake of meeting hardly ever produces an effective meeting.

Figure 1.2 Sample Staff Meeting Agenda

Sample Staff Meeting Agenda

Time	Topic	Person/s Responsible	Preparation Needed	Action or Type of Decision	Desired Outcome
8:00	Gathering, greetings, announcements, adoption of agenda	Principal	Prompt arrival and adherence to meeting norms	Motion to approve agenda	Consensus
8:03	Parent Welcome Committee	Committee members (list them here)	Committee to prepare survey results (see attached)	Staff review of data	Improved parent welcome practices
8:10	Social studies curriculum mapping	Principal	Social studies teacher manuals	Overview of process and determination of grade-level volunteers for district work	Staff awareness and selection of grade-level representatives
8:25	Nuts and bolts Talent show PTA fundraiser Afterschool program coordination	Principal	Previous staff bulletins	Sharing of information; delegation of responsibilities	Understanding of expectations
8:35	Code of conduct	Food service staff	Monthly list	Recognition of exemplary display of manners	Student recognitions by all staff
8:40	Adjournment				

Backup facilitator _____

Timekeeper _____

Recorder and distributor of minutes _____

1.20—CHECK MAIL AND MESSAGES
AT LEAST THREE TIMES DAILY

Learn to communicate using an e-mail intranet within the school campus and district. Paperless communication via e-mail is effective, less expensive, and more rapidly disseminated—only if the school staff is trained to regularly check for messages. Require a minimum of three reviews of the inbox each day—by 9:00 A.M., noon, and before the end of the workday. Avoid curiosity and the tendency to run to the computer every time an audible sound indicates a new message. Turn that feature off!

However, not all communication can be disseminated in a paperless manner. There will always be mail, handwritten phone messages, handouts for staff and parents, and special deliveries placed in staff mailboxes that need to be picked up and attended to regularly.

When the PTA president places fundraising brochures in staff mailboxes mid-morning for distribution later that afternoon prior to dismissal, she doesn't appreciate finding copies in teachers' mailboxes the next day.

1.21—ESTABLISH THE SCHEDULE
AND GOALS FOR THE DAY

In their college classes, teachers would expect professors to provide a course syllabus and a class-by-class listing of assignments, tests, and

WHAT TO DO?

Establish an area in each classroom where an outline of the daily schedule can clearly be seen. Included with it should be a listing of future deadlines for long-term assignments and dates of upcoming tests. Students should be taught how to legibly record this information in their homework planners. Teachers must check to assure this organizational task is learned, takes place each day, and meets a standard of expectation.

In some schools, an assumption may prevail that it is a waste of teachers' time to guide student completion of detailed assignments in planners. Some staff will argue that parents won't read or appreciate the importance of a schedule. Others might argue that primary-aged students are too young to understand a schedule. Perhaps, but the children's parents are not. They appreciate knowing what is happening in their child's classroom. They will notice the classroom schedule when they visit. They appreciate teachers that are structured, organized, and routinely inform them about what is going on—and what is expected from them.

other important information. Why should there be any less planning, organization of content, or communication with students (and parents) in elementary and middle schools?

> **We are all captains of our own ship, but no captain sets sail without a navigator.**
>
> —Noah benShea (2000)

CONCLUDING THOUGHTS

Each school will have numerous other focal points that should be addressed by all staff members to assure consensus of opinion and uniform understanding and fulfillment of expectations for getting each day off to a smooth start.

Typically, there are three influential groups among professional staffs that can limit others' ability to establish structure:

1. The principal or others within the administrative team who fail to establish a vision and clear expectations

2. The "old guard" among staffs that typically shut the doors to their classrooms, fail to work with a team, have differing levels of expectations, and show little interest in assuming responsibility for reflection and school improvement

3. The "rookies" who may or may not understand the importance of structure. Their ideas and habits are still in formative stages and sometimes not aligned with best practices of the school's operation. They need encouragement, support, and a safe environment to make mistakes, grow, and learn best practices.

Utilize the checklist on page 38, as well as those in subsequent chapters, as a guide to reflect on and assess the organizational cohesiveness of a school, to determine strengths and weaknesses, establish goals, and assess current practice in your setting. The checklists can be used as a means to summarize and reflect on the key points described in each chapter. They will help the reader or study groups determine what is applicable or not in other settings and identify other components for unique school environments. The practice of analyzing adult performance behaviors and establishment of site norms will improve productivity and make the work environment better for everyone.

EXPLANATION OF THE STRUCTURAL ANALYSIS AND ASSESSMENT CHECKLISTS

Master Level: Proactively, the entire school staff continuously discusses specific details of structural issues, analyzes strengths and weaknesses in various settings, teaches structural concepts to students in various settings, understands the interconnected relationships between issues, and agrees upon norms of adult and student behaviors. Such behaviors are observable each day. Qualitative measures of school climate and productivity are exceptionally high and sustained over time.

Structure is observable continuously each day.

Professional Level: In response to problems, the school staff discusses specific details of most issues, analyzes strengths and weaknesses in most settings, teaches structural concepts to students in most settings, understands the interconnected relationships between most issues, and agrees upon most norms of adult and student behaviors. Such behaviors are observable most of the time. Qualitative measures of school climate and productivity are high and sustained most of the time.

Structure is observable most of the time each day.

Inconsistent Level: In response to problems, the school staff discusses specific details of some issues but not all, sometimes analyzes strengths and weaknesses, and periodically teaches structural concepts to students in most settings. Different levels of agreement of norms of adult and student behaviors exist. Desired student and adult behaviors are observable some of the time. Qualitative measures of school climate and productivity vary. The entire school staff would benefit from professional development.

Structure is observable each day from some, not others.

Ineffective Level: It is seldom that the entire school staff discusses any type of structural issues, analyzes strengths and weaknesses, or teaches structural concepts to students in various settings. Inappropriate student and adult behaviors are observable each day. Time is wasted. Qualitative measures of school climate and productivity indicate low morale, dissatisfaction, and underachievement. The entire school staff is in need of assistance. Professional staff development from an outside, independent source is recommended.

Inappropriate observations are made each day.

Not Observable: Evidence that the entire school staff discusses any specific details of structural issues, analyzes strengths or weaknesses, teaches structural concepts to students, understands the interconnected relationships between issues, or agrees upon norms of adult and student behaviors is not observable. An issue may not be observable or applicable because of the uniqueness of a setting or other issues.

Observations of structure are not made or are not applicable.

Checklist 1—Beginnings: Structural Analysis and Assessment

Goal	Indicators	Master Level	Professional Level	Inconsistent Level	Ineffective Level	Not Observable
1. There is an effective supervision plan for students before school.	• An adequate number of adults are in place to supervise students. • Plan includes accommodations for weather. • Plan allows physical play time for children. • Adults interact with children and teach expectations. • A trained, effective Safety Patrol exists. • There is an active student council. • The school operates from a mission and with supportive vision statements.					
2. There is an effective plan for greeting parents and students.	• Parent welcome signs are visible. • Staff members speak to parents. • Staff members know names of students and parents. • Teachers greet their classes at the gathering area door. • Preventive problem solving is observed. • Phone calls and messages are responded to each day. • Student incentives are observable.					
3. The supervisory plan focuses on teaching positive behaviors and meeting student needs.	• Staff supervises lines effectively. • Students respond quickly and appropriately to directions from staff. • Minimal time is wasted moving students from one point to another. • Movement through hallways is quiet and orderly. • Organization is evident.					

Goal	Indicators	Master Level	Professional Level	Inconsistent Level	Ineffective Level	Not Observable
	• Home-school communication plans are in effect. • Breakfast is provided. • A dress code is enforced.					
4. There is an effective plan for safety and security.	• Play space is routinely inspected and meets safety standards. • Doors are locked and unauthorized people prevented access during school hours.					
5. The vision of morning supervision and common expectations are communicated.	• Vision and expectations are communicated in various forms by principal. • Morning announcements are made. • Parents are made aware of expectations. • Parents are welcomed at school. • All staff cooperates to avoid wasted time. • Staff behavioral norms are positively observed.					
6. There is evidence of staff planning and adherence to norms of structure and organization.	• Effective meetings are conducted. • Data shows that an effective IAT process is in place. • Grade-level planning occurs and achieves desired results.					

Summary Notes:

(Continued)

Checklist 1 (Continued)

Identified Norms of School Structure:

Areas of Strength:

Targeted Areas for Improvement:

Adult Behavioral Norms Needed to Achieve Expectations:

Recommendations:

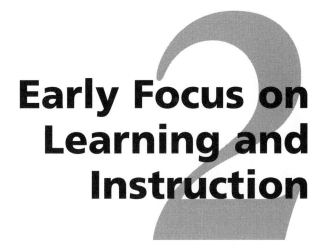

Early Focus on Learning and Instruction

Recommendations for Positive Adult Behaviors That Lead to Higher Levels of Instruction and Student Achievement

INTRODUCTION

Once the morning bells have sounded, the students and adults have settled into their classrooms, and the school year is under way, other considerations for developing and sustaining an effective school organization become the focus. Do all the adults have a common understanding and expectation of what it means to actively engage students in learning? Do all students feel like they belong at the school? Is instructional time being maximized rather than lost to unexpected distractions? Do substitutes know the expectations for the classroom? Do they know when and how to refer students to the office? Do all staff members adhere to a level of mastery utilizing volunteers, supervising students outside their classrooms, administering a code of conduct, and planning effective lessons?

What follows in this chapter, for individual and group consideration, is a sampling of structural issues that might occur during the early parts of the day or year that can potentially impede, or support, teachers' capacity to deliver engaging lessons and effectively manage their students.

Imagination is more important than knowledge. Knowledge is limited. Imagination encircles the world.

—Albert Einstein

We learn by doing real things.

—George H. Wood (1999)

In many respects, teaching and learning are matters of breaking through the barriers—of expectation, of boredom, of predefinition.

—Maxine Greene (1995)

2.1—ESCORT STUDENTS TO AND FROM SPECIAL CLASSES

Good lessons should not be interrupted by excessive noise or disruptions from unsupervised students in the hallways. Over time, every minute of lost learning can compound into lower test scores. Teacher supervision of students while moving to and from special classes should be established as a building norm.

WHAT TO DO?

Teachers should habitually walk their students to and from music, art, media, physical education, and other special classes, effectively supervising students and reinforcing expectations along the way. Punctuality should be observed. Nothing irritates a special resource teacher more than other teachers' inability to watch a clock. Don't allow your lack of punctuality to take away instructional time from others.

Regular classroom and special education teachers must work together to assure an effective transition of students between their instructional areas. Often, the school's most challenged students are "pulled out" and left alone to move distances through corridors. It shouldn't become the principal's job to deal with problems these children get themselves into during this time. Eliminate the loitering. An effective plan for exchanging students saves precious instructional time and reduces the stress of addressing inappropriate behaviors for everyone. An inclusion plan in which the special education is "pushed in" rather than having the students "pulled out" can achieve optimum results.

Want to know where other huge amounts of instructional time are really lost? The answer—moving students between departmentalization setups. Unless all teachers are in sync, the wasted time that students experience standing in a hallway while another teacher completes a lesson can add up. Three minutes each day becomes fifteen minutes in a week, or an hour each month, or more than one full day of instructional time within a year! Even if everyone is in sync, a lack of efficacy in exchanging students can add up just the same.

Don't lose track of time. Teachers who complain that they have an inadequate amount of instructional time must first assure they aren't wasting it!

"Get Your Work Done, or You'll Miss P.E.!"

In some schools, teachers deny students who fail to complete work or adhere to behavioral standards the opportunity to join classmates in physical education, music, or art classes. There should be a revolt from resource teachers about this practice. The integrity of their special class is demeaned when a teacher arbitrarily decides when a challenged child can or cannot attend. Principals contribute to lowering the status of special classes when this practice is allowed to exist.

Likewise, music, art, physical education, and other resource teachers should not send students who misbehave in their classes back to the regular classroom as a form of punishment. What is just is fair in return.

A Lesson Learned

Thomas was a 150-pound fourth-grade student. He epitomized the problems experienced by many lethargic, overweight children. He moved slowly and completed little work; however, he was very likeable. Concerned about his large size, his teachers had pushed for a special

(Continued)

(Continued)

education placement rather than retention when his third-grade reading scores fell far below proficient standards.

Mr. Daniels, the fourth-grade teacher, was concerned about Thomas's reading ability but relieved that he left his classroom for remedial work in Ms. Hartwell's resource room. Preoccupied with students who demonstrated more initiative, Mr. Daniels hadn't noticed the amount of time Thomas spent hanging out in the downstairs hallway or the stairwell on his return to his second-floor homeroom. Thomas loitered in the restrooms, read bulletin boards, stared inside primary classrooms, and drew pictures on the walls during his daily walk. He'd entertain himself and put off returning to the classroom where he didn't feel he belonged and that he thought was boring.

One day, Ms. Bright, the principal, decided to conduct a fire drill at the same time of Thomas's daily leisurely stroll. Spotting Thomas in the hall, she asked him to hide with the custodian in the receiving room.

As the students and their teachers gathered outside, Ms. Bright asked for an accounting of classroom attendance. When all teachers indicated that their students were present and standing in line, Ms. Bright said, "Well, if all our students are standing in these lines, how can Thomas Wright be seated inside with Mr. Workman, our custodian?"

Extremely embarrassed, Mr. Daniels acknowledged his oversight. Never asked to be accountable during drills before, all the teachers learned an important lesson. After this, class lists were always present during emergency drills (see Section 1.13 in Chapter 1). Always have your class list nearby and know where your assigned students are in case of emergency.

Nothing else needed to be said about Thomas's habitual loitering. Teachers quickly tightened their hallway supervision and transitory movements of all students.

2.2—ESTABLISH PROCEDURES FOR RESTROOM BREAKS

Sometime between homeroom time and lunch, everyone needs a break. Principals know, however, that these break periods, if not well supervised, become times when students play around and misbehave, resulting in increased office referrals. Even though the teacher may need a break as well as the students, the responsibility for supervision is never less at the restroom—it is more!

School staffs should establish supervisory norms for this daily occurrence during their back-to-school work sessions. Do this each year. The principal and veterans can teach the beginners, and everyone will be on the same page.

A new principal can learn about past practices and, if needed, further clarify expectations. Revisit the norms several times throughout the school year to refresh common expectations and address concerns. Some expectations that might be adapted to fit your school follow:

WHAT TO DO?

- Develop a schedule of mid-morning restroom breaks so that all classes won't congregate in a crowded corridor, overload the facilities, and waste time.
- Teach students to wash their hands and place used paper towels in waste containers.
- Teach students to flush toilets and urinals.
- Teach students to use inside voices while in restrooms.
- Avoid sending all students, of either gender, into a restroom, out of sight, at one time.
- Be selective about which students are allowed in the restroom at the same time. Don't allow bullies an opportunity to do their deeds!
- Develop an orderly and quick process of allowing students in and out of the restroom while others are washing hands and getting drinks. Send students into the restroom at staggered intervals or in small groups and expect them back in a reasonable amount of time in the same order. Teach them to avoid loitering and mischief.
- Make sure hand soap is available in the restroom.
- Adults should not hesitate to step inside the restroom of their gender to observe student behavior and compliance with expectations. If men are few in numbers at your school, ask for help from the male custodians, paraprofessionals, or volunteers.
- Make sure substitutes are aware of the plan and effectively follow it.

There is no doubt that one or more students will have special needs and require more frequent usage of the restroom. However, when a substitute teacher is present, it seems that nearly all the students suddenly have special needs. Develop a common practice and set of procedures that are uniformly followed throughout the school. Communicate this norm to all staff, substitutes, volunteers, and parents.

Don't allow restroom breaks to become a time for problems to develop or valuable instructional minutes to be wasted. Rather, continue engaging students in a lesson in various forms while the restroom routine takes place.

2.3—PRACTICE ENTERING AND LEAVING ASSEMBLIES

Vendors that routinely visit schools to present programs or deliver speeches will often observe the student and staff entrance and preparation for the assembly. Various individuals can share stories of schools they serve where they were hardly able to speak over the noise from inattentive students. The presenter likely formed a poor impression of the control and influence the principal and staff possessed in that school. The students, who are perhaps not to blame, unfortunately acted as students will without structure and high expectations. Vendors then leave with an unfortunate opinion of the school. Some choose never to return.

Practice entering and leaving assemblies with dignity and respect for guests. Teachers can teach expectations and practice alone with their students. Restroom visits can be conducted beforehand. There should be no need for students to talk, wear hats, bring items to the assembly that might distract others, or interrupt. Selectively place students next to each other who know how to behave, pay attention, and sit independently. Position special needs students near adults. Avoid public address announcements. Disconnect unnecessary, annoyingly loud bells.

In many schools without auditoriums, students must sit on hard, tile, multipurpose room floors. The custodial staff should assure the floors are clean and the room is at a comfortable temperature. The assembly should be scheduled to allow adequate time for room setup and tear down. A good assembly should be interesting, educational, and interactive, never exceeding the attention span of the audience.

The principal, or designee, should monitor students and staff during the entrance period. Praise good behavior and expect to observe more. Once everyone is settled, graciously and enthusiastically introduce the presenter. Staff should remain for the assembly and model good listening skills. Teachers should not be seated in the back of the room grading papers or talking among themselves.

At the conclusion of the presentation, the principal should make remarks of gratitude toward the speaker and encourage students and staff to show their appreciation with applause. Any important announcements can be shared prior to dismissal to classrooms. The principal and staff should assure students leave in a respectful manner.

Expect compliments when your students meet expectations. Realize that vendors will pass on the good news to colleagues in other schools.

2.4—DEVELOP A SUBSTITUTE HANDBOOK

If your school doesn't already have a handbook for substitutes, including all certified and classified positions, develop one. Have plenty of copies available so the receptionist, school secretary, counselor, supervisor, assistant principal, or principal can provide each substitute with one to keep. Along with the handbook should be some form of identification for a substitute (perhaps called a guest teacher) that can be worn and visibly spotted by others. It is only courteous to welcome substitutes and assure that their questions are answered and that they can successfully fulfill expectations. A handbook can help with that process.

Contents of a substitute handbook can include

- A building or campus map
- A staff roster with positions and room assignments
- The name of the head teacher(s)
- The bell and class schedule and work hours for adults
- Common restroom procedures and behavioral expectations
- Student lunch and cafeteria procedures
- Playground supervision expectations, code of conduct, and rules
- Lists of special staff duties and how to fulfill expectations for each
- Emergency information explaining drills, plans, and procedures
- Passwords for computers
- Explanations/locations of adult needs (staff lounge, adult restrooms, lunch costs, contact people, time sheets, etc.)
- Dismissal procedures, bus lists, parent pick-up procedures

Each teacher and staff member should keep an updated substitute plan book in a location easily found by a first-time sub. Many vendors and textbook companies have ready-made lesson plans that could be made available for emergencies. The teacher's substitute plan book must contain all pertinent information about the classroom procedures and the students. Pictures are helpful.

Most important, there should be clear, detailed lesson plans for the substitute to follow listing your expectations for their work, student management, and assessment.

2.5—TIME ON TASK

As part of a multifactored evaluation, school psychologists are often required to observe a student's attention span and record time-on-task work habits within the current least restrictive environment. What they sometimes discover is that a teacher's distractibility contributes to the student's difficulties with time-on-task requirements.

It is impractical to prescribe any standard for adult or student time-on-task behaviors in this volume. However, it is strongly recommended that every professional staff spend time discussing this topic, develop performance standards and norms, and continuously monitor and reflect on practice. Mentors must work closely with mentees to assure efficacy with time management. An in-depth investigation into classrooms or schools with low-achieving students will likely unveil weaknesses in the adults' ability to stay focused. Other weaknesses are inconsistency of expectations, inappropriate utilization of time, and failure to teach each grade level curriculum that is aligned with assessments.

2.6—ESTABLISH INCLUSION PRACTICES

What does an effective inclusion practice look like? Why is it so difficult to develop a common understanding of best practices related to access and inclusion of special learners in the regular curriculum?

First, for effective inclusion to achieve positive results, the entire professional staff must develop a common desire to succeed, a philosophy of acceptance, and a sense of shared responsibility for all learners so that it will work. Anything less is a scheduling arrangement that is just called "inclusion" in name, not in fact.

Second, each child's learning style and individual needs should be assessed, and that consideration should not be limited to those with special needs. All children might benefit from opportunities throughout the day where they are taken out of the regular class and provided enrichment or remediation in small groups. Driven by learners' needs, not the daily scheduling convenience of adults, individual children should experience a variety of pull-outs and push-ins, a fluidity of movement between teachers that effects less awareness of individual labels and "turf" among staff.

Third, every adult must be willing to make a valuable contribution and feel connected with the school. Inclusion will not work if classified personnel feel they are second-class members of the school staff. Most important, inclusion is not working if there is even one staff member who insists on shutting the classroom door and adhering to a practice of strict self-containment.

Finally, inclusion cannot succeed if the principal, or any regular classroom teacher, allows deep-seated beliefs to motivate placement decisions, location of instruction, or responsibility for special learners to be placed upon others.

> **Rank does not confer privilege or give power.**
> **It imposes responsibility.**
>
> —Peter Drucker (2001)

A Success Story

Shortly after Emma and her husband had moved to Pleasantville, she was hired to become the special education teacher of students placed in an emotionally and behaviorally challenged unit being moved to Pleasant Elementary School. Robert, the principal, had requested the relocation of the unit despite resistance from some of his veteran teachers.

As the school year began and new students were gradually assigned to the unit, there were some difficult transitions. Several of the students attempted to continue exhibiting the behaviors that had brought them attention in their home school. Adjustments were difficult. But Emma, her paraprofessional assistants, and regular classroom teachers eventually developed a smooth routine within her highly structured resource room as well as the students' regular classrooms.

The students, mostly very troubled young boys assigned from other schools, raised concerns from many staff members when they first arrived. Regular classroom teachers took special note of who they were. The anxiety level among the staff was high as they waited for the boys to create disruptions and problems at "their" school.

But that never happened. Their angry behaviors and emotional breakdowns subsided within weeks as they all fell in love with their teacher—and she with each of them. Eventually, they blended in with other Pleasant students and steadily made gains and achieved goals listed in their Individualized Education Plans (IEPs).

What contributed to Emma's and her students' success? A positive attitude and attention to structure. Emma never considered excluding her students from anything. They attended regular and resource classes, assemblies, parties, and other special activities whenever they were appropriate and determined to be the least restrictive environment for their learning. The students adjusted and succeeded most of the time in their regular classrooms. Her "boys" became steady learners when they knew they were welcomed and loved in the safety and security of her classroom and elsewhere at Pleasant Elementary School.

2.7—ESTABLISH PROCEDURES FOR REFERRING STUDENTS TO THE OFFICE

Does it bother you if a principal says, "Good teachers hardly ever send students to the office"? It may be true that those who are skilled at motivating and engaging their students rarely find it necessary to send students to the office, but kids are still kids. Despite best efforts, there are important reasons why kids should occasionally be referred to the office. Here are a few:

- *Personal injury or sickness.* If there is blood, the principal and office staff should know about it. If a child is sick, the nurse should be consulted. That doesn't mean a free pass or automatic office visit for any child who complains of an ache or pain. When that is allowed, every child who is bored in class will be afflicted with aches and pains.

- *Illegal or illicit behavior.* If the teacher suspects drugs, weapons, theft, or other violations of the school district's conduct code, the principal should know. Protecting a child or failing to investigate can be negligent—and disastrous.

- *Overt refusal to follow an adult's directions.* No child has the right to ignore reasonable directions from an adult. The problem in implementing this guideline is establishing a commonsense level of understanding and tolerance among adults.

- *Danger or threat to other students.* Children should not have their right to learn in a safe environment threatened by others. The best teachers sometimes have challenging students in their classrooms that require a more restrictive environment. Create an inclusive environment, but never allow one kid's bad behavior to spoil it for the others.

Certainly this list is not comprehensive. Yet, it can serve as a guide. Effective teachers learn how to pick their battles within the classroom, continuously teach expectations, utilize their extensive repertoire of motivational techniques, know when to ignore, and engage most of the students all the time. They know that when they let down their guard, the kids will take advantage. When that begins to happen routinely, it should not be the principal's job to fix the problem. Over time, principals will learn the problem they have to fix rests with the teacher, not the kids.

2.8—FULLY UTILIZE VOLUNTEER SERVICES

Volunteers are special people who provide immeasurable resources to a school. They are deserving of great respect and gratitude. How their time is structured, managed, and assessed is an important consideration that should not be left to the discretion of individual staff members. Where there are systems in place to identify needs, solicit volunteers, train them, and listen to their concerns and ideas, volunteerism will flourish.

When developing a volunteer program, establish a guide or handbook. It should include

- A list of common expectations and information available to all guests at the school
- Detailed information outlining time frames and the work or service to be provided
- Expectations related to background checks and confidentiality
- Information contained within a substitute handbook that would be pertinent to a volunteer

Nothing will discourage the spirit of volunteerism more than the staff's failure to plan and prepare on a daily basis, establish clear expectations from the start, provide feedback, and be honest and accountable. Volunteers want assurance that their work is appreciated and contributing to a common good. Otherwise, they will feel their time is wasted.

Don't allow the contributions of volunteers ever to go unrecognized, even if some of them prefer otherwise. Volunteer recognition events need not be costly or extravagant—nor should they be limited only to annual events. The point is that every professional staff should find numerous ways to continuously express their gratitude to volunteers both individually and collectively.

2.9—TEACH A CODE OF CONDUCT

Typically, teachers want to know the new principal's plans for *discipline* of their students. In reality, what many want to know is whether the new principal will *punish* students for inappropriate behavior or lack of effort. In a school culture where punishment is strictly equated with discipline, productivity is likely to suffer. Discipline suggests teaching; punishment implies something negative.

WHAT TO DO?

Read Dr. Ruby Payne's (1996) *A Framework for Understanding Poverty.* In it, she describes the excessively loud noise levels that are common within homes of families living in poverty. In light of her research, how can a teacher insist that a poor child be punished for being loud in the classroom? If foul and inappropriate language is all that a young boy hears at home, it's easy to understand why he might use the same vocabulary at school.

Historically, one of the purposes of schools has been to instill middle-class values among diverse groups within the American public. To best do that, the focus has to be on teaching rather than punishing. Kids must be taught how to socially act and respond to daily situations. They must be allowed to make mistakes and learn better choices. Once lessons have been taught and mastered, there should be consequences for bad decisions. This is nothing different from what your mother probably taught you.

If adults in your school routinely have to raise their voices to be heard, yell, lose their temper, or shout and say "shut up!" at children, a code of conduct is needed.

The posting of classroom rules is a requirement and good practice in schools. However, when that list of rules becomes so long that it can't be recited, you likely have too many rules. Keep your rules short and simple—and limit the list to a few (such as how to work and respond to questions, maintain safety and personal space, show respect, and treat others).

A code of conduct is about more than rules. It is a summation of a set of standards, common expectations by which everyone in the school—students and adults—are guided and governed. The code of conduct addresses the common values necessary for a good work ethic, the attainment of quality work, integrity, honesty, safety, courtesy, respect, and treating others kindly. For success, every child must learn these values. They must be reinforced continuously. "Words of the Week" are meaningless if the children and adults never internalize the important concepts and positively change behaviors. Where a code of conduct is established, taught, and firmly rooted in the culture of the school, when problems do occur, it is much more effective to ask a child, "What part of *our* code of conduct did you fail to follow?" rather than immediately blaming and criticizing.

Adults, including parents, must continuously model the code of conduct. When that happens, adults demonstrate socially acceptable behaviors. Children will learn from example and follow positive role models, and long lists of rules will then become unnecessary.

The two things that move a person out of poverty
are education and relationships.

—Ruby K. Payne (1996)

Rationale for a Schoolwide Student Management Plan and Code of Conduct

Schools must be safe and productive.

School staffs must create a climate with a high expectancy of student success.

Students must be motivated and engaged.

Staff must be guided to prevent problems and view those problems that do occur as *"opportunities for teaching."*

2.10—COMMON, GRADE-LEVEL PLANNING INCREASES STUDENT ACHIEVEMENT

Negotiated contracts often dictate the amount of planning time allowed for each bargaining unit member. How that time is spent, however, is determined by the individual. Master teachers recognize the power of collective experience and wisdom and create ways to plan together. The best results are achieved when all the teachers providing instruction for a particular grade level, including special resource teachers, plan for instruction and assessments together.

WHAT TO DO?

Teachers that effectively plan together by common grade level do the following:

- Agree upon a common meeting time, develop an agenda, determine desired outcomes, establish effective meeting norms, and assign specific roles and tasks. That meeting time might be at 10:00 A.M. if students can be scheduled with resource teachers or in other activities.
- Utilize a variety of data to drive instructional decisions, such as benchmark and chapter tests, standardized tests, writing samples, and observations.
- Create a curriculum map, if one doesn't exist, that is aligned with the district course of study and mandated tests. The map should list the essential concepts and standards that must be taught and learned at proficient levels by students.

(Continued)

(Continued)

> • Invest in staff professional development activities and consultants that produce results. When fully empowered, outside consultants can confront the sacred cows, such as long-standing methodologies, curriculum content, scheduling preferences, groupings, or pacing. They also provide the expertise that insiders cannot. The well-known adage that one cannot be a prophet in his or her own land seems especially relevant among educators.

Teachers who plan together and stay together eventually get results and enjoy coming to work. Two heads are better than one. It is much easier to paddle a boat with several oars in the water than just one alone.

> **Education is what you get from reading the fine print.**
> **Experience is what you get from not reading it.**
>
> —Anonymous

> **If you want children to put their feet on the ground,**
> **put some responsibility on their shoulders.**
>
> —Abigail Van Buren

CONCLUDING THOUGHTS

Chapter 1 dealt with structural concepts that could be planned and implemented at the beginning of a school year or day. In contrast, Chapter 2 focused mostly on structural issues that support teachers' instructional practices and management of students within classrooms and areas of the school where they move about in groups or alone. Statements made in this chapter and throughout the book imply that higher levels of productivity are attainable when individual management capabilities are aligned with schoolwide adult behavioral performance norms.

Furthermore, many of the essays and stories affirm that teachers play a key role in enabling children to be successful. Teachers that struggle to control students in their classrooms demonstrate varying degrees of incapability promoting their students' success. Today, more than ever before, teachers must be better prepared and far more advanced when assuming responsibilities in their classrooms. They must be equipped with a repertoire of instructional methods and strategies that effectively address the diverse needs of each student. Teachers must reduce gaps and challenge the brightest simultaneously. Those can be foreboding tasks for an individual with little experience keeping 25 young students focused and continually motivated to complete tasks at hand.

DiGiulio (2000) described three axioms for student success and positive classroom management:

1. Students who feel successful are seldom behavior problems.

2. To feel successful, students must actually be successful.

3. To actually be successful, a student must first do something of value.

It may be difficult to distinguish between individual classroom success and schoolwide performance. There must be an analysis of results considering each. Inside the classroom, the teacher is often the lone adult. There, the vision, expectations, and goals must be expounded by the teacher, not the principal. Success of students is the teacher's foremost goal. Students must recognize the teacher as the authority. When teachers fail to establish positive connections, students will challenge and act out. If the teacher is unable to handle challenges alone, the students will quickly surmise that he or she lacks backbone and control. In total, the school may achieve admirable results, but as part of the whole, the potential success for one class can be placed very much at risk.

The instructional dimension of teaching is likely what entices young people to enter the profession. Most want to emulate the image of a favorite teacher. That's a noble goal, but likely unattainable when the structural and physical dimensions of school business are misunderstood or ignored.

Checklist 2—Learning and Instruction:
Structural Analysis and Assessment

(See explanation of the structural analysis and assessment checklists at the end of Chapter 1.)

Goal	Indicators	Master Level	Professional Level	Inconsistent Level	Ineffective Level	Not Observable
1. Classroom instruction is engaging, motivating, and inclusive.	• Classroom teachers "wow" students, parents, and visitors. • Labels and turf issues are nonexistent. • Student behavioral problems are minimal. • School is quiet during instructional hours. • There are positive results from the implementation of a code of conduct. • Awareness of time on task is observed in classrooms and elsewhere. • Grade-level team planning occurs weekly. • Data shows that structure contributes to higher levels of student achievement. • Challenged students have specific behavior plans that work.					
2. There is an effective plan for substitutes and volunteers.	• Handbooks are available. • Detailed plans and job descriptions are available and followed. • Staff members know names of substitutes, welcome them, and assist. • There is evidence of planning and feedback for volunteers.					
3. There is an effective plan for supervising students in the hallways and restrooms.	• Staff supervises lines at restrooms effectively. • Students respond quickly and appropriately to directions from staff.					

Goal	Indicators	Master Level	Professional Level	Inconsistent Level	Ineffective Level	Not Observable
	• Minimal time is wasted moving students from one point to another. • Movement through hallways is quiet and orderly. • Organization is evident. • Little time is wasted between resource classes. • Attention and behavior at assemblies is exemplary.					
4. The reasons for office referrals are minimal.	• Teachers are empowered to effectively manage classrooms. • Students view all teachers as authority figures. • A sense of order, consistency, and cooperation among staff is observable. • A code of conduct is reinforced.					

Summary Notes:

Identified Norms of School Structure:

(Continued)

(Continued)

Areas of Strength:

Targeted Areas for Improvement:

Adult Behavioral Norms Needed to Achieve Expectations:

Recommendations:

Midpoints of the Day and the Year

*Ideas and Advice That
Provide Students With Structure and
Positive Behaviors When Needed Most*

> **A good structure during lunch and recess will ensure
> continued success and harmony the rest of the day.**
>
> —Paul Young

INTRODUCTION

A typical school day may be moving along without incident when suddenly, during lunchtime, for no apparent reason, everything seems to come unglued. Likewise, after a strong start at the beginning of a year, momentum begins to slow and problems surface more frequently at midyear. After sorting out and dealing with problems caused by students or parents, experience has it that a common explanation for the disruptions will emerge. Principals know that when students or adults are in less structured settings, problems are more likely to occur.

During the transition from morning instructional block to lunch and recess, much of the responsibility for supervision of students transfers to other adults, sometimes paraprofessionals. When those in charge fail to assume those duties, perform ineffectively, or perceive that the children under their watch are another person's problem, cracks in the overall school structure begin to emerge. Students seem to be able to sense these lapses, and typically if you "give them an inch, they will take a mile."

Because it is also time for their lunch break, parent visits increase. If the receptionist, secretary, or other office staff members fail to be at their stations, some parents, even though they might know better, unabashedly walk right past the office and proceed to other areas of the campus. It only takes one, loose, disgruntled parent in the building to create an unsafe and chaotic experience for *all* the students and adults.

Effective staffs realize that the lunch and recess periods are when their organizational structures become most susceptible to problems. They also know that good planning reduces the potential for trouble to develop. When the adults are performing well and effectively supervising students, fewer behavioral problems will require immediate attention and resolution after recess. In addition, the return to the classrooms for the afternoon instructional block will go much better.

3.1—EQUIP YOURSELF FOR PLAYGROUND SUPERVISION

All staff members should keep a folder or clipboard in a convenient location and carry it with them each time they report for playground supervision. At a minimum, that clipboard should contain

- A current list of the students to be supervised according to grade and assigned teacher
- Playground rules, guidelines, and supervision expectations
- Office referral forms
- Discipline referral forms
- Emergency plans
- Safety gloves
- Pictures of challenging students
- Pictures of any parents (or others) who pose a threat to security
- Pencils, pens, and notepaper
- Paper clips
- Band-aids
- A whistle
- A "Red Card"

A "Red Card" includes your name and a simple message such as

There is an emergency on the playground.
   Please alert another adult to inform the office staff and come quickly to assist.

At first awareness of a developing crisis, the supervising staff member gives the Red Card to a reliable student with instructions to run to find another adult. Red Cards are critical forms of communication when time or conditions limit other options.

In this age of technology, adults supervising playgrounds should have access to a reliable system of voice communication with the school office. This might consist of a walkie-talkie, two-way radio, cell phone, or other convenient and reliable form of communication. Be mindful that some two-way radio systems transmit beyond the confines of the school and may be monitored by citizens in the surrounding neighborhood.

If allowable in your setting, small digital cameras or camcorders can be helpful to record and document problems or concerns. Review your district's policy on photographing students.

Plan and prepare. It may appear cumbersome to take a folder with you to the playground, but planning, training, and proof of preparedness will serve you well in the event of an emergency or a serious challenge from a disgruntled parent.

3.2—TEACH MANNERS AND HYGIENE

Once lunchtime arrives, the relative quiet of the morning instructional block turns chaotic in some schools. The same successful instructional approach with students that fosters classroom achievement can be sustained throughout the lunch and recess hour—if the adults don't let down their guard.

At all times, especially at lunch, manners and hygiene should be taught. Structure the rotation of classes through the cafeteria so that all students have time to use the restroom and wash their hands before they eat. Hand washing with soap and water, not only before lunch and during restroom visits but also at other times throughout the day, will help minimize the spread of communicable disease. But children will not always wash without adult reminders. Entire classes of children will avoid this routine if the teacher doesn't allow time for a stop at the facilities before arriving at the cafeteria.

While waiting in line for food, students should be adequately supervised and taught to remain in their own personal space using inside voices. Students, just as much as adults, should be allowed to talk during lunch time. However, children have a tendency to speak louder than adults. Without structured limits, the noise level in cafeterias will escalate out of control. All staff in the vicinity of the cafeteria must share responsibility for teaching and reinforcing appropriate levels of group conversational talk—in a pleasant, respectful manner.

Teachers should assure that each child understands appropriate manners in the lunch line. Students should be taught to make eye contact, speak in complete sentences with food service staff, and say please and thank you when receiving a lunch. Students will become used to this daily routine over time, and the habit will become part of their persona when eating out in restaurants.

3.3—FACILITATE EFFICIENT FOOD SERVING LINES

Many schools are using computerized systems for tracking and maintaining data about students' participation in the lunch program and recording lunch money transactions. Typically, students are given an identification number that can be entered into a keypad or a card that can be swiped electronically like a credit transaction. Some programs allow parents to prepay for lunch online and monitor their child's account and eating patterns. These contemporary systems, sometimes considered too expensive by officials in smaller schools or districts, likely pay for themselves over a short time by providing better data (which generates more profit), requiring less time to process individual transactions, providing concerned parents with valuable feedback, and eliminating the stigma and easy identification of free or reduced lunch participants in the federal lunch program.

Regardless of how meals are served and money collected, the principal should establish a process that is conducted with efficiency. Too often, lunchroom duties and responsibilities are delegated to classified staff members that lack experience, training, and influence to initiate needed improvements. An effective principal knows that his or her presence in the cafeteria sets the tone for common expectations. The principal must establish a common vision of expectations and monitor others' ability to fulfill them. Otherwise, expect long lunch lines, impatient and bored students misbehaving in line, wasted time, financial deficits, and an ineffectual school lunch program.

Following the principal's lead, teachers should take their students to the cafeteria at the beginning of the school year and practice "lunch." It doesn't hurt to have refresher sessions throughout the year. Consider the learning needs of the students that join classrooms midway through the year. The youngest children need to hear and see everything they need to know about the lunch process. They need assistance from adults who patiently explain where to select and receive a lunch, what to say and do, how to choose and acquire extras, how to pay, where to sit, what to do if items are forgotten, and how to speak with others and display good manners. As lunch ends, students need to know how to pick up trash around them and on the floor and deposit waste properly.

When adults take the time to teach and model expectations, and stay at it for a period of weeks, everyone will enjoy an immediate positive impact on students' behavior at lunch.

3.4—SCHEDULE RECESS FIRST, EAT AFTERWARD

Based on numerous observations, it appears to be common practice in elementary and middle-level schools that lunch is always scheduled first, followed by recess. However, a common concern from adults observing students in that setup is that many children gulp food, or don't eat at all, so they can rush to a game on the playground. Attempting to help students learn better and develop relaxed eating habits, some staffs have achieved positive results by reversing the schedule. Some noticeable outcomes from that practice are

- Less wasted food—students worked up an appetite with exercise
- Better variety of foods selected
- Less digestive concerns—the number of office referrals for students playing too hard on full stomachs drop
- A more relaxed eating atmosphere
- Fewer conflicts carried into the classroom after lunch—children return ready to learn

Implementing a change in a typical lunch and recess schedule requires good planning and time to realize results. The physical location of some school's cafeteria and playground may present different challenges for student supervision when the schedule is reversed. The time and procedure for hand washing may need to change. New considerations for the placement and convenient storage of carry-home lunch boxes, toys, coats, and boots must also be well thought out. It is meaningless to change one schedule if it becomes disruptive to others in the school.

Most likely, the students will quickly adapt to whatever schedule is established, especially when they receive good training. Resistance to a change in the midday schedule is more likely to come from adults—concerned parents who feel left out of decision-making processes and insecure staff who always adhere to the status quo.

3.5—SPEAK WITH INSIDE VOICES

Young children can learn to speak with inside, *sotto voce* (Italian musical term for *under the voice*) voices. They can learn to distinguish and differentiate the type of vocal volume that is appropriate for physical education classes as well as the library. Some adults might prefer that children be seen and not heard (as from the old adage), but that doesn't help them develop social skills or learn appropriate ways to raise the dozens of questions that they are innately driven to ask. It is essential for an orderly school involvement, and preparation for real-life functions, that children learn to temper the loudness of their voices at appropriate times. In addition, adults need to assure that proper eye contact is being made when individuals speak to other people, whether the conversation is initiated by an adult or student.

Most often, children are loud because they are excited and enjoying themselves. However, adults should also recognize that students will be loud when they are modeling what they've observed. Moreover, the voice levels of children will increase most when they are begging for attention.

3.6—PRACTICE FORMING LINES

Teaching students to safely and quickly form a line isn't easy. Depending on what event is being anticipated, students' enthusiasm to get to the next experience might create an abundance of supervision issues for the teacher. It takes time and practice for students to know what to do. But if they aren't taught or if teachers can't envision or communicate expectations, confusion creates problems and sometimes accidents and injuries occur.

WHAT TO DO?

Lines are formed at all times of the day. Good instruction and monitoring from the start of the day sets the tone for expectations at other times. What follows are some little considerations that, when taught and implemented, can produce effects of smooth line formation.

- Assure clear egress to the designated area. Remove clutter and book bags from the areas where students need to walk.
- Quickly and clearly state your expectations before allowing any individual or group of children to move. Never give more than three directions at one time. More than that will not be remembered.
- Encourage students to orally repeat the directions. This can be helpful from time to time.
- Invite small groups at a time to move from their location to the point the line will form.

- When they are seated, teach students to stand quietly, push their chairs under the desk or table, and to walk (not run) quietly to form the line.
- Designate a line leader who is the class foreman. Make it a prized, powerful, weekly classroom job. That student must assure that all students comply with the teacher's expectations and directions. If it is less than satisfactory, the foreman can request the line be shaped again. If this happens often, the students will realize they are wasting time and will work together as a team to move forward.
- Selectively assign placements in line for difficult students or bullies.
- Besides the line leader, assign a line caboose. That designated student is always last in line. Make it an important "job" for students. They'll think they are important when they get to be the caboose. Once in the hallway, the teacher can always identify the point of the end of the line.
- Teach kids that, as with trains, when distance between cars (children) becomes too great or too close, the line breaks, and the train derails.
- Teacher proximity and effective supervision of lines reduce the potential for problems. Most student discipline problems in lines occur if, and where, the children think the teacher can't see.

Often, student teachers are assigned to a supervising teacher where the line formation routine occurs so effortlessly and well that it might be taken for granted. As a result, the student teacher enters the profession without the opportunity to observe firsthand the details and strategies utilized by a master teacher to structure the process. Unless this process is quickly mastered when you first are assigned your own classroom, others' observation of your classroom management might be less than positive. Don't allow the principal to observe this weakness during his or her first observation.

Lesson From the Field

Timmy and Tommy, fourth-grade identical twins, needed no other names in their school. All the teachers knew about them—and dreaded the thought of ever seeing either name on their class lists. "Little devils" was a term used to describe them.

(Continued)

(Continued)

Despite the fact that both were bullies, very ornery, and seemingly always in trouble, Timmy and Tommy were bright little boys. Actually, they were much more observant than some of their teachers. Theirs is a story about teaching their teachers the importance of monitoring and supervising lines.

They had been plotting their "escape" for days. They knew and understood that there was a regular rotation of teachers assigned to supervise the afternoon recess. They also knew which teachers had a watchful eye and which ones did not.

As they had brilliantly observed, Mrs. Hooper was the least effective at playground supervision. On the days she was assigned to the playground, they had their way with the other kids and could do what they pleased without ever getting caught. Timmy described it best: "A statue could watch us on the playground better than Mrs. Hooper!"

So, inspired by the escape scenes they watched in movies and television dramas, they plotted a getaway from their rural playground, bordered by a farmer's cornfield, for a sunny October afternoon before fall harvest.

Like prisoners planning a breakout, Timmy and Tommy knew that Mrs. Hooper never looked back at the line of students once she directed them to walk the 100 yards from the playground to the school. Their scope and view of the sidewalk from the end of the line, awareness of obstructing trees, and Mrs. Hooper's ineffective supervisory capacity contributed to their confidence in carrying out a clear getaway.

The escape was planned for the day before Halloween. As they had hoped, it was a warm and sunny afternoon. When the bell rang at the end of recess, they purposefully went to the end of the line. There they threatened kids who might squeal who watched what was about to happen. Mrs. Hooper blew a whistle, got the students quiet, gave some directions (which few could hear), and from the front of the line, began escorting the students into the school—never looking back.

Timmy and Tommy saw their moment at hand. They jumped the fence, hid in the corn rows, camouflaged themselves with dirt and mud, and waited until all the students and Mrs. Hooper were inside.

It was an hour before Timmy's and Tommy's teacher, Mr. West, realized they were absent without leave. He had assumed they were playing another of their practical jokes. He was near panic when he realized the principal was at a meeting, a substitute secretary was struggling to manage the office, and the custodian was also a substitute. As critical time passed, Mr. West became increasingly worried for the boys' safety and called the local police. Mrs. Hooper, on the other hand, seemed unconcerned, failing to grasp the potential seriousness of the situation.

Timmy and Tommy thoroughly enjoyed their freedom. They walked and ran five miles through farmers' fields and woodlands to their rural home. There, they played, climbed trees, and hid from view when they spotted Mr. West and the local constable driving past their house in search of them.

A great tragedy might have occurred had the boys been picked up by a stranger. But luckily nobody messed with Timmy and Tommy. When notified, their mother wasn't the slightest bit concerned or worried about their welfare. She knew they'd return home when they got hungry or it got dark. And sure enough, they did.

The next day at school, the principal felt obligated to teach them a lesson they would never forget. Whatever was said or done was probably soon forgotten, but a longer-lasting lesson about supervising the line after recess was learned by all the teachers—taught by Timmy and Tommy.

3.7—STRUCTURE PLAYGROUND GAMES

If there is continuous conflict and tension on your playground (created by students, not adults), it may be time to address those issues and develop a plan to achieve better results.

Unfortunately, too many teachers dread the days they are assigned to supervise the elementary school playground. Some never understand that close observation and a preventative approach can eliminate many problems. Others simply grin and bear it, put in their time, complain in the lounge about the students' behavior, and hope for an alternative duty assignment.

If approached differently, with planning focused on students' interests, playground supervision can actually become a pleasant, refreshing, and relaxing experience for children as well as adults.

WHAT TO DO?

1. Make sure there are adequate numbers of adults assigned to the playground to assure proper supervision and that the play space is limited to an area that can always be within view.

2. Utilize parent volunteers. There should never be less than two staff members on a playground.

(Continued)

(Continued)

> 3. Develop a schedule of games and activities that students will enjoy.
>   In consideration of students' varying ages, try organizing some of
>   the most common:
>
>   • Kickball
>   • Softball
>   • Races
>   • Jump rope
>   • Hopscotch and four square
>   • Cooperative, noncompetitive games using parachutes, earth balls,
>   beanbags, balloons (Orlick, 1982)

There should be no limit to what can be scheduled, and a varied
weekly schedule will add interest. The point is to simply better organize
games and activities and allow students a choice. Where there is structure, with the supervising teachers reinforcing expectations and actively
engaging students in activities, there will be a reduction in fights, less confusion and debate over rules, fewer excluded students, and hardly any
tears. Students can move in and out of games and activities of their
choice. To promote healthy exercise habits, all students should be involved
in some sort of movement. When they burn off their excess energies,
they'll return to the classroom refreshed, relaxed, and ready to learn.

3.8—MONITOR STUDENTS' BEHAVIOR AND EATING HABITS

Eat with the children! They are fun to be with and won't gossip or gripe
about your colleagues like many adults will in the staff lounge.

Actually, many teachers do invite students to eat with them. They
arrange private lunches, engage in lively conversation, listen, and learn
much about the child that might otherwise not have been shared. The
child leaves feeling a special connection with the teacher.

When adults have responsibility for lunchroom supervision, they
should be observant of students' eating habits. Much can be gleaned that
may provide key insights and explanations about other problems. Identify
picky eaters. Notice the children that throw most of the lunch away—
then appear hungry later. Observe the variety of foods that parents or
children pack at home to eat at school. Who shares their food and displays
manners? What choices are being made from the school lunch offerings?
Who spends a lot of money on a la carte items and not the lunch?

Distinguish healthy eaters from others. Who still appears famished? Identify students who talk and socialize and those that do not.

A positive presence of teachers and staff members in the lunchroom will help facilitate student movement and student compliance with rules. To avoid problems, and a letdown of the structure, all adults must assume responsibility for success—even if it is their break time.

3.9—ESTABLISH PROCEDURES FOR INDOOR RECESS SUPERVISION

In a majority of schools, rainy days force students inside during recess. Because of space limitations, students are often placed in classrooms for indoor activities. However, negotiated agreements often stipulate uninterrupted lunch opportunities for bargaining unit members and the availability of adults for supervisory duties is often less than the number of classrooms needed to place children.

Without a schoolwide structural plan and specific guidelines and attention to supervision, indoor recesses can present numerous concerns and problems, quickly becoming the most at-risk period of the school day. It is just as important to plan and establish supervisory expectations for indoor recess as for the playground.

WHAT TO DO?

1. Teach expectations. Kids need to know their parameters. Let them know what they can play with, where, with whom, and how loud their voices should be.

2. Assign seating and play areas. Some kids will be more physical than others. Good teachers proactively make specific seating assignments and structure play areas for challenged students before they leave the room.

3. Provide children with a variety of games, exploratory and enrichment center–based activities, and computer programs that engage students while reinforcing academic skills. Other ideas to effectively occupy time might include

   - Educational videos and DVDs (combine classes for easier supervision)
   - Board games (checkers, chess, etc.) that can be played individually, in pairs, or in small groups
   - Drawing and arts and crafts activities

(Continued)

(Continued)

- Computer access
- Blackboard games
- Cooperative games
- Assignment of paraprofessional assistance
- Prearranged visits and access to the school library or music room
- Storytelling conducted by volunteers
- Private, sustained reading opportunities
- Seat and floor exercises

There is no limit to what can be imagined, planned, and implemented. Where there is good planning and expectations are continuously reinforced, problems are minimized. Where there is an increase in squabbles and subsequent office referrals during inside recess, the structure is weak. Reflect, evaluate, and plan for more effective outcomes. Plan, do, study, then act on results!

Now, what about eliminating recess? Reacting to pressures to increase instructional time and raise student test scores, many principals and their staffs have chosen to reduce students' recess or physical education time—or even eliminate it. Those decisions appear likely to boomerang in light of demands that schools address the childhood obesity crisis. Remember to keep perspective and balance. The ideas presented in this book, if implemented, should help teachers regain the instructional time they typically lose dealing with miscellaneous student management issues that occur when cracks in organizational structure emerge.

3.10—TAKE PICTURES AND USE RECORDERS

School policies often include parent or guardian authorization and permission for a variety of special events and activities: bus field trips; walking field trips; Internet access; and identification and inclusion of students in yearbooks, photographs, publications, Web sites, and so forth. Know your policies and follow them.

To support an effective schoolwide structural plan, teachers and adults should have ready access to digital cameras and recorders. These tools can be used to effectively document behavioral incidents. As the saying goes, "pictures don't lie." A photo or a recording from the scene of an incident helps save time that otherwise might be devoted to distinguishing students telling the truth from those who are not. Students' awareness that they may be recorded can have a positive impact on negative behaviors. A student choosing to yell, scream, or curse might think twice when he or she realizes Mom or Dad might be able to listen to a recording of the incident later. Tape recordings can make kids as well as adults eat their words. For security reasons during afterschool hours, many school officials install outdoors cameras that monitor high-risk areas. These also increase security during the school day. Cameras have proven to document problems and reduce behavioral disputes on school buses and at key bus stops. Invest in and utilize technologies that support school structure and student management.

More controversial, perhaps, is the use of cell phones. Many come equipped with cameras. They provide immediate access to help during emergencies. They also provide immediate access to parents—and parents with access to their kids. Their usage can be both positive and negative. They can disrupt classes. They can be misplaced or stolen. Regardless, cell phones are becoming increasingly more prevalent.

Many boards of education have developed policies (often accessible online) that permit video security cameras to be used on school buses and playgrounds. The policies, and the rationale behind them, likely are varied, but they generally are designed for the purpose of improving student discipline and assuring the health, safety, and welfare of everyone. Every school staff must continuously consider what is needed to assure student welfare. It is prudent to collaboratively develop administrative policies that clarify the widespread utilization of cameras, recording devices, and cellular communication technologies. Make sure that all laws, regulations, and policies allow such practices and that parents and other stakeholders are informed of the school's plans.

3.11—ESTABLISH CONTINGENCY PLANS FOR CRISIS SUPERVISION

If your school is fortunate enough to employ paraprofessionals to supervise the cafeteria or playground, is there a contingency plan if they cannot report for duty? What if an assigned staff member suddenly becomes ill? Is there an emergency plan that is immediately implemented that provides for the care and supervision of the ailing person's students?

It is probably impossible to imagine or plan for every type of problem or emergency that might occur. However, common sense dictates that every possible attempt to assure safety and security of students and adults must be made. Every school staff member should be aware of several predetermined safe havens where they should calmly relocate students in the event of an extended building evacuation. They must also have plans for supervising students and communicating with parents and each other during unforeseen, stressful situations.

Good training contributes to effective responses to emergency situations. Regularly practice the routine emergency drills. *Recognize that schools are most vulnerable during lunch and the middle part of the day* while there are numerous academic/recreational/academic transitions and increased levels of visitation during the public lunch hour. Develop plans for who should be consulted, what should be done, and how students will be managed when confronting situations such as the following:

- Threats from intruders
- Intimidation of staff from bullying parents
- Fights between parents
- Custodial battles
- Choking, heart attacks, unconsciousness
- Sudden death of a student, parent, or staff member
- Reports of serious accidents involving parents
- Student attack or injury of a staff member
- Police interrogations of students or adults
- Child protection services interrogations
- Loss of power or water
- Gas leaks
- Neighborhood fires, emergencies, or evacuations
- False accusations against staff
- Takedowns and restraints of children that are out of control and a danger to others or themselves
- Children that run away from school

Everyone on your school staff needs to know how and when to call 9-1-1. However, from among the numerous things that might be happening simultaneously as a crisis develops, that is usually the most easily recognized and obvious decision. Other decisions may be trickier. Training helps. A staff that effectively works as a team to analyze and improve day-to-day organizational issues can handle most crises in a professional manner. Crises and emergencies will happen, and when they do, individual grit and true colors will be exposed. Let your colors shine!

3.12—TEACH CHILDREN TO SPEAK IN COMPLETE SENTENCES

How many times have you asked a child a question about why they did this or that, and the answer was, "Because." Even though "because" is considered a standard American English response in casual register, it doesn't demonstrate an expansive command of vocabulary. Because textbooks and tests are written in formal language, the importance of practicing complete-sentence responses can reinforce classroom instruction. In particular, if the child's family speaks a nonstandard American English dialect, or are nonnative speakers of English, they might benefit greatly from repetitious practice of arranging thoughts in complete, proper sentences.

The middle part of the day, during lunch, recess, and other breaks, is an ideal time for adults to engage students in conversations, model appropriate speaking skills, and insist that skills learned in the classroom are practiced in the freedom of social settings. What are some of the benefits?

- Reinforcement of correct grammar. The child will hear and learn that it is incorrect to say, "That boy *don't* like pizza!" or "Billy *had went* to the wrong door." The ability to self-correct can have a direct correlation to higher test scores when that same child has to read a story and select right answers from distracters.
- Reinforcement of the skills taught in classrooms related to identifying and using nouns, verbs, adjectives, and adverbs.
- Expansion of vocabulary. Speaking in complete sentences helps the teacher and child focus, practice, and improve language usage together.
- Better oral skills. While listening, the teacher must encourage proper eye contact, appropriate vocal volume and inflections, and other nuances of speech. Children also become better accustomed to speaking to adults and each other.

Musicians know that the ability to perform lyrical phrases correctly, to make aural sense, and to convey the composer's deep meaning and message requires extensive practice. So does learning to speak a language.

So why should a school staff consider this tip? It is a sound strategy that enriches student-teacher interactions. It reinforces language instruction at all times of the day where learning may not be the primary focus. Speaking in complete sentences, when modeled and consistently reinforced throughout a school from the beginning of the day to the end, can contribute to higher test scores. Where the structure is such that every adult expects and helps students learn to speak in complete sentences, appropriate use of language improves. It requires effort and commitment from all adults, but it works!

Help Children Gain the Verbal Advantage

Every child will at some time be asked to respond to a teacher's question, give an oral report, speak on the phone, or converse with adults. Most likely, a student's formal learning eventually culminates in a job interview. The ability to speak effectively in that important setting provides the listeners with an immediate impression of the interviewee's background and educational level. Being poised and able to speak effectively can sometimes be more important than the ability to pass a written test.

What to Do?

To help children gain the verbal advantage, parents and teachers can work together in the following ways.

• *Insist that children speak in complete sentences.* Starting sentences with "because" or answering questions with a shoulder shrug does not help students gain an advantage. When they slip, utilize a signal that reminds them that they must self-correct. When an entire school community buys into the importance of correct language usage, the united effort will help not only the children, but also the adults, develop a verbal advantage.

• *Build vocabulary.* Reading teachers have lists of basic words that all children should recognize and understand for success in each grade. Ask for the lists and make sure *all* children know them and can relate them with learning experiences outside of school.

• *Model appropriate speaking skills.* Children enter school reflecting the oral language skills and use of casual register they have heard in their homes and environment. But while at school, students must learn and practice the formal registers of written and oral language. All staff and child care providers, regardless of background or level of education, must model high standards of oral language. Develop innovative questions that will become conversation starters. Enjoy teaching and conversing with the kids.

• *Make eye contact when speaking.* Mumbling or avoiding eye contact can lead to negative first impressions.

• *Use correct grammar.* Young children who learn to say "It *don't* get any better than this" will find "It *doesn't* get any better than this" to appear strange on standardized reading tests.

• *Avoid slang, colloquialisms, unnecessary sounds, and incomplete words.* There is no doubt that in many situations, being able to speak in a casual manner can help make a point. But children need to learn to distinguish between casual and formal register, and use them appropriately. Using slang inappropriately can be embarrassing in formal settings. Modeling how to finish suffixes (such as "going vs. gonna" and "reading vs. readin'") helps lay the foundation for the verbal advantage. Interviewers rate those who muddy their spoken language with numerous "you knows" or "uhs" lower than those who speak correctly.

- *Help children avoid bad habits.* Graduates that can't structure a sentence without using the word "like" place their youthful fad in stark comparison with peers who speak correctly and with maturity.

- *Teach the importance of pronunciations, volume, and tempo.* Young learners model what they hear at home and school. Mispronounce words or speak too quickly or softly, and likely the children around you will as well.

- *Seek professional help early.* Consult with school officials and request a screening for pronunciation problems that persist beyond normal stages of development.

- *Encourage your students to speak in front of large and small audiences.* Encourage children to participate in plays at school and church, to memorize poems and stories, to talk at the dinner table, and to take advantage of talk time in the car. Model public speaking for children and listen.

- *Encourage parents to monitor TV usage.* Parents must observe what their children watch on television, and turn it off if the language is incorrect or inappropriate. Television, without controls, can be the source of many bad oral habits.

The world's best leaders are great orators. They learn not only what to say but how to say it well—accurately and with confidence. To become leaders of their generation, young learners must gain an oral advantage.

Parents are the first to teach their child to talk. The first words are a memorable time in a child's development. That development must continue for a lifetime as an individual works for mastery of the oral language. The formative years in school are critical for later maturity. Parents must be involved and work closely with school officials, establish high expectations, model speaking, and listen. Children who achieve the oral advantage will reap rewards in a multitude of ways throughout their adult lives. That is a magnanimous gift to give to children.

3.13—DEVELOP A CONFLICT MEDIATION PROGRAM

Inevitably, conflicts develop on school playgrounds. Despite the negative connotation, interpersonal conflicts are important in developing social skills and coping mechanisms. All students (and adults) will benefit from learning about the causes of conflict and resolution strategies. Conflict mediation programs provide students with a sense of self-empowerment.

Unfortunately, many effective conflict mediation programs fade away when adults become preoccupied with other activities or lose interest. Student conflict mediation programs require adult supervision and facilitation. For long-term success, a staff must be committed to planning, reflection, evaluation, and continuous improvement.

WHAT TO DO?

Consult with your local mental health agencies or social workers for help in acquiring materials and instructional guides for starting conflict or peer mediation programs. Likely, they have trained personnel that can provide special programs or consult with school staff and empower them to deliver instruction. Talk with colleagues in other schools for their recommendations. Court officials also have resources they can share. The Internet contains innumerable sites related to the topic, such as

New Jersey State Bar Foundation: http://www.njsbf.com/njsbf/student/conflictres/elementary.cfm

Indiana University: http://www.indiana.edu/~safeschl/resources_mediation.html

University of Nebraska: http://www.ianrpubs.unl.edu/epublic/pages/publicationD.jsp?publicationId=147

National Youth Violence Prevention Campaign: http://www.violencepreventionweek.org/index.html?menu=resources&l=3

CONCLUDING THOUGHTS

If you ask young children to identify what they like most about school, a popular response will be "lunch and recess!" In contrast, adults may choose lunch as a favorite time, but they are less likely to include recess with that same answer.

Staffs that perform at the master level understand the pitfalls of supervision and student management that detract from a smooth, organized school operation. They focus on teaching expectations, prevention instead of reaction, positive attitudes instead of negativity, and shared responsibility for school success. They do not experience the common avoidance syndrome found in many schools. Adults say "Let me help" rather than "That's not my responsibility right now."

Without a doubt, there are many other midday and midyear issues that will be unique to various school sizes and locations and that require adult attention. This chapter is intended to be a springboard for helping the reader focus on and identify those situations and determine strategies for increased effectiveness. This kind of planning makes for a pleasant and educational midday or midyear experience for everyone.

Checklist 3—Midpoints: Structural Analysis and Assessment

(See explanation of the structural analysis and assessment checklists at the end of Chapter 1.)

Goal	Indicators	Master Level	Professional Level	Inconsistent Level	Ineffective Level	Not Observable
1. The lunchroom is efficient, orderly, and enjoyable.	• Classroom teachers and paraprofessionals effectively supervise students in lines and while eating. • Students observe rules of good manners and hygiene. • Student behavioral problems are minimal. • Lunchroom inside voices are appropriate. • There are positive results from the implementation of a code of conduct. • Technology is evident that supports efficacy. • Students eat a balanced, nutritious lunch.					
2. There is an effective plan for moving students from the lunchroom to the playground or vice versa.	• Attention is paid to forming lines. • Safety is observed at all times. • There is evidence of planning and input from all staff. • Staff behavioral norms are observed.					
3. There is an effective supervisory plan for students during outdoor or indoor recess.	• Varied communication needs are addressed. • Emergency planning is evident. • A variety of activities for students is planned. • Minimal time is wasted moving students from one point to another. • Movement through hallways is quiet and orderly. • Organization is evident. • Little time is wasted between recess and afternoon instruction. • Teachers greet their students at the playground after recess.					

Goal	Indicators	Master Level	Professional Level	Inconsistent Level	Ineffective Level	Not Observable
4. Teachers and paraprofessionals interact and communicate with students in a positive manner.	• A code of conduct is reinforced. • Students and adults speak in complete sentences. • Conflict is acknowledged and resolved peacefully. • A sense of order, consistency, and cooperation among staff is observable.					

Summary Notes:

Identified Norms of School Structure:

Areas of Strength:

Targeted Areas for Improvement:

Adult Behavioral Norms Needed to Achieve Expectations:

Recommendations:

The Second Half of the Day and the Year

Ideas and Advice That Produce Positive Outcomes for Learners of All Ages

INTRODUCTION

Naps after lunch were nice in preschool. They used to be common in kindergarten and primary grades, but times have changed. Demands for higher accountability and increased student achievement have forced most staffs to abandon those practices. Perhaps the pendulum may swing back someday, and that may not be all bad. Regardless of your thinking, students typically have the ability and vigor to do what the teacher requests. The problem is that an unspoken concern persists—too many adults lack the stamina to teach with intensity and enthusiasm through an entire day, or the full school year. It is difficult to sustain interest through midday or midyear slumps and humps. Moving beyond with vigor and enthusiasm can be challenging. The series of topics discussed in this chapter, and others that readers will identify for their school, are presented to support these critical periods of time in school.

4.1—READING CAN BE TAUGHT AFTER LUNCH

Most elementary teachers prefer a schedule with an uninterrupted block of time for teaching reading and language arts activities, preferably in the morning. Scheduling disputes sometimes erupt when primary-level teachers are asked to conduct reading or language classes after lunch. Why? Many teachers fail to recognize that reading is taught across the curriculum throughout the day. During science and social studies classes, students are reading. In music classes, students read. Everyone should read continuously throughout the day.

The purpose of including this topic in this chapter is not to extend the debate about when intensive, focused reading skills should or should not be taught. Instead, the point is to suggest a topic for passionate teachers to discuss as part of a schoolwide organizational plan. Instead of arguing about which teacher has the more ideal schedule to teach reading, it would be better to discuss and debate the following questions:

1. How much do students read when outside their classrooms? Are students encouraged to read signs in the cafeteria? The hallway displays? Office bulletin boards? The outdoor marquee? Does anyone assist those who struggle when outside the classroom?

2. Are grade-level reading skills and vocabulary lessons reinforced by the music, art, and physical education teachers? Are these teachers and other resource personnel included in grade-level planning meetings (see Chapter 2, Section 2.10)?

3. Is the entire staff successfully planning the integration of reading skills throughout all other areas of the curriculum? What is the evidence of results?

When a staff effectively deliberates how best to maximize the use of time each day, week, and month, it becomes clear that reading must be taught continuously—by everyone. That may require a paradigm shift, but such a focus directs students toward positive activities and reduces the amount of time they might engage in undesirable pursuits.

4.2—CREATE AN "ADAM PLAN"

Despite your best efforts to prevent it, some students gain a notorious reputation that they cannot shake. When a problem develops on the playground, they seem always to be there. They are blamed for incidents when sometimes, in reality, it was the fault of others. Yet, because of damaged self-esteems, nothing these children try to do appears to put them on the right foot. They lack the social skills and self-discipline to keep their mouth shut and hands to themselves. When the teacher looks the other way, they antagonize their peers—or so they stand accused. When the principal investigates, "Adam" always seemed to provoke others out of sight and earshot of adults.

Tightly structuring the movements of such a child to avoid situations where physical and verbal contact with peers takes place will reduce problems—and provide the challenged child with a respite from detentions or other consequences. As an example, teachers must team closely to maintain the required close proximity with these children, because, literally, "Adam" must be allowed no time throughout the day where his interactions with peers are unobservable or unheard by adults. If a conflict does occur, a teacher is there to quickly mediate and resolve it. Bullies who may have enjoyed initiating problems and then deflecting blame toward "Adam" learn to play somewhere else, and the accusations by other students will likely stop. The one-on-one attention from an adult can have immeasurable positive effects on "Adam."

The "Adam Plan" works best when other students are unaware of the reasons why he is always in proximity of an adult.

Staff buy-in and detailed planning are essential to the success of this plan. But the results can be measured by less time resolving nuisance conflicts, improved attitude and reputation, and increased academic gains—for both "Adam" and his peers.

> **Nothing effective happens in an elementary or middle-level school without the endorsement and support of the principal.**
>
> —Paul Young (2004)

4.3—SUPERVISE STUDENT SUSPENSIONS

Commonly, board of education policies delineate procedures for student suspension. Unfortunately, there are few consequences or options that lead to positive results with the most challenging students. Particularly in elementary schools, the intended outcomes of student suspensions always seem overshadowed by the trouble they create for adults. Teachers and principals tend to worry about the lost instructional time and lack of supervision for a young child placed out of school. For an in-school placement, finding an adequate location that can be well-supervised can become a challenge. What follows are some do's and don't's for supervising student suspensions.

WHAT TO DO?

- Follow board-adopted policies when suspending children.
- Utilize the services of all resource and support personnel to intervene with challenging students.
- Involve the parent in developing a plan to change behavior.
- Place the suspended child in a designated room or area that is bright, warm, and continuously supervised.
- Schedule a child in other teachers' rooms or with paraprofessionals, or utilize trained volunteers when other staff members are unavailable.
- Allow the child to eat lunch in the in-school suspension room.
- Document inappropriate behaviors presented by a student with cameras or tape recorders.
- Assure that all children's due process rights are respected.
- Follow up and make sure all pertinent staff members are aware of the suspension and its effect and expectations for their work.

WHAT *NOT* TO DO

- Don't fail to fully explain the problem, the consequences, and gain parental support.
- Don't place the school's most unruly students in public view. Don't give visitors a reason to talk about the negative behaviors of your students.
- Don't expect the school secretary or custodian to fulfill supervision requirements.
- Don't create an in-school suspension area in a small closet. This constitutes cruel and inhumane treatment.
- Don't prevent any child from routine use of the restroom.
- Don't take away a child's lunch privileges for failure to work or lack of compliance.
- Don't place a child in a location where there will be numerous distractions or access to confidential information.
- Don't wait until faced with a serious situation to develop a schoolwide plan.

The entire school staff must share responsibility for the development of a plan for supervising suspensions. Teachers' responsibilities for children are never suspended—just the student's opportunity to participate in class with others.

4.4—WRITE NOTES AND RETURN PHONE CALLS

Every teacher realizes that there is very little free time in a typical teaching day. It seems there is always more to do, not less. But two daily routines should never be overlooked, whatever the work load may be—writing personal notes and returning phone calls.

Every good mentor instills these habits in his or her protégé. The act of writing a personal thank-you or congratulatory note demonstrates that you sincerely want to show gratitude, acknowledgment, or recognition for another's acts. Write three of them each day.

WHAT TO DO?

- Send a note to the nursing home director thanking him or her for sharing supplies.
- Thank the superintendent and principal for their support.
- Thank the PTA for their assistance.
- Congratulate a colleague on a special lesson he or she presented.
- Thank teachers for covering a duty for you.
- Send notes to students commending them on their accomplishments, especially activities outside of school.
- Recognize volunteer contributions.

The returns on the investment of time and cost of stationery will be well worth it. Teach kids to do this same routine.

If a parent, student, vendor, or community patron calls and leaves a message, his or her reason for calling must have been important. Don't go home until every attempt has been made to return each of those calls. Don't procrastinate. Don't let important matters stall. The adage that "those who snooze will lose" is true. Capitalizing on opportunities that originate from phone calls requires immediate action, not getting to it some other time when it's convenient. Of course, responding to e-mail, especially from parents, is just as important as addressing a phone message. Check to see if your district has an expected or required response time for e-mail.

When you make a telephone call and get placed "on hold," use the time to begin writing one of your three daily notes.

4.5—TEACH MULTIPLE INTELLIGENCES

Students learn in various ways. That statement explains why all the little boys and girls who grow up to become drummers in their bands couldn't resist making noise by tapping out a beat with their pencils at the desks. The theory of multiple intelligences helps explain why many athletes are so talented manipulating their bodies, other people are so quick to recognize words, and still others grasp complex mathematics concepts with ease.

In too many classrooms, students are asked insufficient numbers of effective questions, especially those that require an understanding of concepts at levels higher than basic recall based on Bloom's taxonomy. All teachers should have access to quick reference guides that contain some question starters that will lead to development of higher critical thinking skills for students. These are available from many sources. Once provided to all teachers, they should be used!

During grade-level planning meetings, teachers should ascertain that they provide more than paper-and-pencil instructional strategies. The hours after lunch and recess are ideal for focusing on all the intelligences as described by Howard Gardner (1993):

- Linguistic intelligence: a sensitivity to the meaning and order of words
- Logical/mathematical intelligence: ability in mathematics and other complex logical systems
- Musical intelligence: the ability to understand and create music. Musicians, composers, and dancers show a heightened musical intelligence.
- Spatial intelligence: the ability to "think in pictures," to perceive the visual world accurately, and re-create (or alter) it in the mind or on paper. Spatial intelligence is highly developed in artists, architects, designers, and sculptors.
- Bodily/kinesthetic intelligence: the ability to use one's body in a skilled way, for self-expression or toward a goal. Mimes, dancers, basketball players, and actors are among those who display bodily/ kinesthetic intelligence.
- Interpersonal intelligence: an ability to perceive and understand other individuals—their moods, desires, and motivations. Political and religious leaders, skilled parents and teachers, and therapists use this intelligence.

- Intrapersonal intelligence: an understanding of one's own emotions. Fiction writers use this intelligence, and counselors use their own experience to guide others.
- Naturalist intelligence: an ability to recognize and classify plants, minerals, and animals, including rocks and grass and all variety of flora and fauna

An infusion of arts can also have a profound effect on student understanding, investment, and ability to meet or exceed the standards. In general, students who study the arts not only do well on standardized testing measures, but do better in real-life measures of learning (Deasy, 2002). They are often capable and confident readers, writers, and users of math. They are strong thinkers and workers. They treat others well.

4.6—SHOW EVIDENCE OF STUDENT LEARNING

If asked to show evidence of student learning, most teachers typically provide test scores or point to papers proudly displayed on bulletin boards. These same professionals complain about high-stakes testing and the measurement of schools' progress based only on an annual, one-shot assessment. Tests, when used effectively, provide good data. But there must be more evidence that students are learning.

First, teach the standards. Then assess in a variety of ways, more than with paper-and-pencil ready-made tests, to assure that each student is progressing with critical thinking–skill development and mastery of key-concept understanding. Some recommended assessment methods include the following:

- Oral or written open-ended or extended response exercises
- Extended tasks—sustained attention in a single work area and carried out over several hours or longer
- Portfolios—selected collections of a variety of performance-based work
- Rubrics—indications of the degree to which something was learned
- Dramatic reenactments and role-plays
- Authentic interviews
- Computer-assisted evaluations

Regardless of the methods utilized, there must be continuous attention and focus on assessment and learning in a highly structured school. Observers will notice that students are excited to share what they should know and can demonstrate that knowledge in a variety of ways. The types of questions heard in effective classrooms include

- How would you select . . . ?
- How would you justify . . . ?
- How would you compare . . . ?

Students' responses show whether they are capable of making informed judgments and comparisons rather than simply recalling basic facts, terms, or answers.

Listen to the interaction between teachers and students in the hallways. Analyze the kinds of questions being asked. When adults challenge each other and model the questioning expected in classrooms, the evidence of learning will increase.

4.7—ALLOW CHILDREN TO DRAW

The Washington, D.C., Arts Education Partnership's 2002 release, *Critical Links*, summarizes the results of 62 research studies that examine the effects of arts learning on students' social and academic skills. The research studies cover each of the art forms and have been widely used to help make the case that learning in the arts is academic, basic, and comprehensive.

Use drawing as a creative intervention. Some kids can listen, learn, and draw at the same time. Many will learn better when they can draw a picture. Those with photographic memories will visualize words, graphs, pictures, and illustrations in their texts. Allow them to draw—it supports an important learning style for numerous students.

Drawing reduces the amount of inappropriate behaviors that accompany boredom.

4.8—SERVE FRUIT AND VEGETABLE AFTERNOON SNACKS

Not long after lunch, many students will be hungry and need a mid-afternoon pick-me-up. Serve fruits and vegetables. There should be some reflection and evaluation of practice in schools where candy is widely distributed by teachers as incentives or a form of bribery to motivate kids to complete their work. Those practices seem contradictory to the local, state, and national initiatives forming to promote healthy eating and fitness habits for overweight children.

No resources or capacity for storage of fruits and vegetables? Ask the PTA to assume responsibility for this project. To promote nutrition and healthy food choices, most parent groups will embrace this idea. If costs are too much for your budget, the offering doesn't have to be available each day, but once the kids (and adults) get used to the benefits of better choices, they won't want anything else.

The Child Nutrition Reauthorization Act of 2004 (Public Law 108–265) amended section 18 of the National School Lunch Act to establish the Fresh Fruit and Vegetable Program (FFVP) as a permanent program. Check to see if your school can qualify for this grant opportunity.

4.9—DON'T GET TIRED AND LET DOWN YOUR GUARD

Principals know, as a typical day nears an end, that healthy teachers have energy to engage children and utilize every minute of instructional time. These individuals are in great physical and mental shape. Yet some begin to run out of gas and sometimes allow the kids to gain the advantage of control. However, the greatest concerns focus on those few that consistently lack the mental stamina needed for effective, sustained performance each day. They are most prone to letting down their guard and allowing problems to develop.

The most common indicators that negatively impact performance are stress and depression. For some, complications from health conditions and medications make them tired. Bad dieting and poor nutrition habits also contribute. Just as with the children, a fruit or vegetable snack might be an important afternoon boost.

Teachers and all school staff members must stay in good shape to be effective. The structure of each school should include a wellness plan—for adults as well as students. That plan can support

- Development of daily individual or group exercise activities
- Tobacco cessation support groups
- Nutrition education
- Weight control support

Runners learn how to pace themselves for races. They also train methodically and take care of their bodies. They know that expending energies too quickly and failing to satisfactorily refresh will affect performance. Teachers must learn those lessons as well.

> **We can never control a classroom**
> **until we control ourselves.**
>
> —Todd Whitaker (Whitaker & Lumpa, 2005)

4.10—GIVE ATTENTION TO CUSTOMER SERVICE

At some point while attending long off-campus meetings, a principal places a telephone call to check on matters back at the school. Doing so, he or she experiences what the public typically does when calling the school. Are the phone lines all busy? Do excessive rings transpire before an answer? Is the call answered by a person or automatically transferred to an answering machine or voicemail? Is the personal greeting pleasant? Does the receptionist use correct grammar? Does the caller obtain a positive first impression of the school?

The receptionist or school secretary plays an important role as point of first contact for your school. When visitors enter the office, he or she should look up and provide a warm greeting. The receptionist must appear confident and competent. Messages must be recorded accurately and relayed to others efficiently.

How are other visitors received and acknowledged in other parts of the campus? All of these questions and observations must be assessed and determined to be positive. The principal sets the tone, and the effective secretary or receptionist fulfills those expectations. The principal must then respect and positively reinforce a job well done!

4.11—ELIMINATE LOITERING IN THE HALLWAYS AND OFFICE

In a well-structured school, it is difficult to find students sauntering through the hallways trying to kill time moving from one room to another. Where that occurs, boredom is likely to be the cause.

Likewise, the school office must be structured so that students do not loiter while waiting for services from the nurse, counselor, social worker, or the principal. Do not allow the students with the worst attitude and behavior to have a "stage" on which to display themselves for your important guests and visitors. Create an area out of view, but supervised by an adult. Don't display dirty laundry when it isn't necessary.

As with any type of customer service, if students are waiting an inordinate amount of time in the office to see an adult, the practice should be studied and remedied. It should not be the secretary's job to supervise unruly children for extended time periods while they wait in the office for another adult.

4.12—UTILIZE HOMEWORK PLANNERS

Good-quality, age appropriate, reasonably priced student planners or organizers are available from numerous vendors, along with a variety of resources for teachers. Easy wipe-off classroom charts provide teachers a means to list all assignments the way they want students to copy them in their planners. When assignments are written clearly and with detail, parents and afterschool personnel can understand them and provide adequate assistance. Effective teachers empower students to help update the assignment list and maintain awareness of the assignments throughout the day. One of the final routines before dismissal should be a whole-class review of assignments with assurance that these assignments are recorded and planners prepared to take home.

The most effective teachers convey the importance of these planners as school-home-school communication tools and take time to teach parents the expectations that both they and the teachers should have for their daily utilization. For example, the planners help kids develop organizational skills. They are also a tool that helps students learn responsibility. Most brands contain interesting curricular facts and sidebar information that reinforce social skill development. As weeks go by, a positive record of teacher-parent communication becomes documented and maintained in these booklets—and the opposite outcome is evident for those, both teachers and parents, who don't communicate. The time devoted to this effort should be minimal and viewed as a method to reinforce many critical skills. Homework planners are a positive method for documenting parent involvement. With time, it becomes easy to identify those parents who spend less time assisting and monitoring their children's homework than others.

A decision can be made to incorporate other methods to achieve similar results—Friday Folders (oversized bags used to help young children organize and carry papers home to parents), online homework help sites, and so forth. The point is, utilize whatever works best for your situation, use it consistently, and make sure to develop parents as partners.

4.13—COMMUNICATE WITH PARENTS

When parents ask their children what they did at school that day, the most typical response is "Nothing." The exchange often leads to frustration and negative outcomes. It seems that the older children become, the more difficult it becomes to talk with them. Young adolescents do like to talk, but not always with their parents—or on demand. Because of the challenges they are experiencing with interpersonal relationships compounded by growth changes, adolescents enter into their own zone, and only the lucky or the most skilled parent seems to be able to get information out of them about school.

To help with that, educators need to structure ways to provide information about what happened at school to parents in writing. Prepare a short written summary of the day's highlights, the major concepts introduced, and the due dates of upcoming assignments and tests. Send it home each day. Teach parents to look for it.

Right away you might be thinking that young adolescents will never get that piece of paper home! Maybe, maybe not. That doesn't mean you shouldn't take the initiative just the same. Viable alternatives might include using e-mail, teacher Web pages, homework help lines, telephone networks, and other written forms of communication besides paper.

Moreover, teach parents how to ask a better question. Instead of asking the open-ended "What did you do at school today?" question, focus better with "What good questions did you (or someone else) ask?" or "What good things did you do today?" or even "Who got into the most trouble today?" These attempts to center on important information you really want to hear about will likely get the conversation flowing.

Most important, help parents affirm. Help them understand the importance of building on children's strengths, not their weaknesses.

CONCLUDING THOUGHTS

Aesop's fable about the tortoise and the hare seems applicable to conclude this chapter. Those in schools who move at lightning pace through the activities of the day often tire like the hare. Instead, a steady pace like the tortoise saves energy for the final part of any race or activity. Students respond well to effective pacing. On the other hand, they'll take advantage of teachers who let down their guard at this critical period. If there are cracks in the wall, they will find them.

Basketball players know that games are won in the second half, not the first. Only those teams with the endurance and energy to persevere throughout the game and season will achieve success.

Teaching isn't any different. Endurance is an important quality of effective teaching, and it is important that students learn to maintain steady and consistent levels of effort throughout each day, all year long.

Checklist 4—The Second Half: Structural Analysis and Assessment

(See explanation of the structural analysis and assessment checklists at the end of Chapter 1.)

Goal	Indicators	Master Level	Professional Level	Inconsistent Level	Ineffective Level	Not Observable
1. There is evidence of student learning.	• All teachers teach reading across the curriculum. • Planning and instruction to meet students' multiple learning styles and needs is evident.					
2. Afternoon instructional periods are as effective as morning.	• Staff members are observed to have energy and enthusiasm. • Healthy snacks are available. • There is evidence of planning and input from all staff. • Staff behavioral norms are observed. • Office referrals are handled effectively. • The number of office referrals maintains consistency with other parts of the day.					
3. There is effective planning for homework completion and parent communication.	• Varied communication needs are addressed. • Emergency planning is evident. • A variety of activities for students is planned. • Minimal time is wasted moving students from one point to another. • Movement through hallways is quiet and orderly. • Organization is evident.					
4. Teachers and paraprofessionals interact and communicate with students in a positive manner.	• A code of conduct is reinforced. • A sense of order, consistency, and cooperation among staff is observable.					

(Continued)

(Continued)

Summary Notes:

Identified Norms of School Structure:

Areas of Strength:

Targeted Areas for Improvement:

Adult Behavioral Norms Needed to Achieve Expectations:

Recommendations:

Endings: Dismissal and Wrap-Up of the Year

*Reflective Advice and Ideas
That Teach and Reinforce
Positive Behaviors as School Winds Down*

Leave no children behind. The staff can relax only after each child is safely released to the care of a parent or designee.

—Paul Young

When students are disruptive in the hallways, office, fields, assemblies, bus zones, or any other building location, the school's reputation, the level of parent support, student learning, and staff morale are dramatically affected.

—Mark Boynton and Christine Boynton (2005)

INTRODUCTION

The school day may be ending, but not the responsibilities of the staff. Experience shows that dismissal can be one of the most dangerous and high-risk times of the day, for students as well as adults. It is essential that the school staff identify the small structural issues that support and facilitate a safe and efficient dismissal of students—before leaving themselves.

To ascertain the validity of that statement, visit schools and watch what happens. Where students exit the school in an orderly manner, adults will be visible. They will be observed greeting parents, talking with bus drivers, planning with afterschool personnel, and releasing students to the care of a parent or guardian.

However, in other schools, many adults appear to be racing the students out of the building in a rush to the parking lot. Who is left to care for the child whose parent is late arriving at school? Who answers questions about homework? Who hears complaints or discusses issues with concerned parents? Which schools appear to place the interest of students first? Where would you rather your child attend?

Likewise, the end of the year is an important time to reflect, assess the success of the school's practices and procedures, and plan for the next year. This takes time. Don't rush. Assure that all the loose ends are tied. Summer vacation will wait. Reflection is an integral part of the planning process. Clean up the messes before starting afresh. Then celebrate the end of the year.

5.1—MONITOR BUS PICKUP AND DROP-OFF LOCATIONS

As mentioned above, one of the most potentially dangerous times of the school day is during dismissal. Typically in a rush, parents driving to school to pick up their children add to the congestion of buses and others walking home. Throw in some inclement weather, and it can be one chaotic mess as everyone seems determined to pick up a child at the front door. Very few school campuses seem to have been designed with traffic flow in mind or adequate parking.

Facilitating the movement of buses on tight schedules quickly in and out of the school campus must be a priority. But be careful! Accidents can happen when children are not closely observed while buses enter and leave. Common safety practices should include

- Adequate adult supervision where buses load or unload. An adult should always stand between the bus door and students.
- A rule that keeps students in a safe area. Students should never be permitted to approach a bus until it reaches a complete stop.
- Continuous reminders that students should never attempt to retrieve books or papers from beneath a bus
- Adult intervention that prohibits late students from running alongside a moving bus
- A location clearly marked "Buses Only" for loading and unloading

Just as prone to danger and accidents are the pickup and drop-off locations scattered throughout your community. Without supervision, older students, unaware of their mortality, often stand extremely close to a busy street and taunt drivers with all sorts of inappropriate behavior and comments. Pickup and drop-off points may be outside the legal responsibility of school officials, but all safety considerations must be evaluated to avoid negligence.

WHAT TO DO?

School officials should

- Clearly delineate in writing the supervisory responsibilities of parents and school officials at all bus stops
- Request and seek parent supervision at all bus stops
- Utilize adult volunteers to supervise dangerous bus stops just as you do at busy street intersections for walking students
- Delegate responsibilities to various staff members to assure that all students and parents are safely out of the building and off school property each day
- Solicit police intervention for repeated severe problems

No matter how much planning takes place, some accidents may be unavoidable. However, risk factors can be reduced and positive community relations developed when school officials are viewed as proactive rather than reactive when it comes to bus stop problems.

5.2—RIDE SCHOOL BUSES

Hopefully, your school community will never experience a serious bus accident. However, tragedies do occur, and awareness of transportation processes and expectations can help make a bad situation better. Visual familiarity with routes, bus stops, and transfer locations; awareness of the students assigned to routes; a study of traffic patterns; and an observation of students' behavior and the amount of time they spend on buses can be helpful both in times of typical business and those of crisis.

Principals and teachers should periodically ride school buses. Whether your school is in a rural, suburban, or urban setting, much can be gleaned from a bus ride with students. You might view riding a bus as outside the scope of your job, but the insights gained about children's lives and routines in your community from the vantage point of the bus will enable you to better appreciate your students and the conditions in which they live. Firsthand knowledge about students' experiences prior to their arrival at school, or following dismissal, can influence numerous other decisions impacting their time at school. Bus drivers will appreciate the acknowledgment of the challenges they face. They'll welcome your assistance and support with student management and discipline. And they'll provide you with new understandings of children, their families, and your community if you listen.

Do you desire better relations with transportation personnel? Want to reduce bus conduct referrals? Just ride, observe what happens, and listen. Principals, especially, should find riding a bus to be invaluable.

> **The only thing harder than managing a bunch of students is to do it while driving a bus.**
>
> —Todd Whitaker (Whitaker & Lumpa, 2005)

Attention to Details Can Saves Lives

Marybeth was a first-year bus driver for Countryview School District. Like other new employees, she had received intensive training from her administrators and valuable advice from her veteran colleagues. Unsure, at times, how some of the advice might be applicable, Marybeth listened just the same and tried to include all the little details that her peers suggested in her work. As she would soon learn, one detail—the ritual of training each student to make eye contact before being motioned across a street in front of the bus—would save a life!

One mid-October Friday afternoon, miles from the school on a country road, Marybeth had stopped the bus to let Richie, a kindergarten student, off in front of his house situated to the left near the road. Just as Richie had reached the spot 10 steps beyond the right front side of the bus, the spot where he was trained to stop, look toward the driver, and wait for the signal to cross the road, Marybeth noticed a large, rapidly approaching garbage truck, apparently out of control and unable to stop. Unaware of impending danger, Richie waited for a signal. With few seconds to spare, Marybeth made eye contact and motioned Richie to jump back into a ditch instead of crossing the road to his waiting mother.

Seconds later, the truck, having lost its brakes, collided with the bus, pushing the engine, accordion-like, back toward Marybeth and the remainder of her riders. The impact pushed the bus 50 yards down the road until it veered off into the ditch. As that happened, a large branch from a maple tree was forced through the back door and came crashing several feet up the center aisle.

Marybeth's training and attention to details saved Richie's life and prevented a horrific situation from becoming even worse. Immediately after the accident happened, Marybeth surveyed the damage, observed there were no serious injuries among her passengers, got them off the bus, and immediately began reassuring them that they were safe. Miraculously, neither she nor her remaining 15 young riders suffered any severe injuries. Her calm handling of students prevented shock and limited their tears. She gave a copy of her accurate bus list and emergency telephone numbers to Richie's mother with directions to call emergency personnel, the principal, and other school officials. Within 15 minutes, parents were called and quickly informed about the accident and its location. They were also reassured of their children's safety and care.

It is unimaginable what might have happened had Marybeth failed to teach and reinforce the very little detail of making eye contact with each student before giving permission to cross in front of the bus. Her attention to detail and quick action saved a life. Yours might, too.

5.3—DELINEATE WALKING STUDENTS FROM PARENT PICKUPS, BUS RIDERS, AND OTHERS

Schools are architecturally designed in different, unique ways. In many, it may be logical (and promote safety) to dismiss students riding buses, walking, being picked up by parents, or remaining for an afterschool program at distinctly different areas. To do so effectively, a teacher or paraprofessional at each grade level should be assigned to escort each group of students to the various dismissal areas and remain there until all students have been safely dismissed. Some advantages of this practice are

- Efficiency in accounting for all students, managing supervision, and assuring that all the correct students arrive at their prearranged dismissal area—and that no student is forgotten in a restroom
- Avoidance of congestion in any one high-traffic area
- Assurance that all children are dismissed and released by a staff member to a custodial parent or designated adult
- Confidence that children will not be going home with unauthorized friends or adults and that all children are picked up

The time invested to guarantee a safe dismissal will allow everyone else, especially the office staff, to complete other work. It will also satisfy parents and lead to a less stressful evening for all.

5.4—WALK STUDENTS HOME

From time to time, surprise parents and citizens within the neighborhood by walking students home. It won't take long, and the public relations established with shared learning opportunities will be memorable. Principals, teachers, and paraprofessionals can learn much by initiating a surprise home visit.

Expect various receptions. Some parents will graciously welcome you; others will not. Regardless, what you might observe and learn about a student's home life will likely influence your expectations. You will no longer chastise a fourth-grade student for failure to complete homework, assuming the child should have completed it at the kitchen table like you did as a child, after you see the child's home has no kitchen! From the simple act of walking students home, many teachers gain insights that influence their planning and structure of the school day—and perhaps the way they look at kids. They then develop interventions and school-based programs that support children during time before or after school for those children who lack adequate support and supervision at home.

5.5—SHARE POSITIVES WITH PARENTS

After walking a student home, create positive public relations by sharing some positives with the child's parents. Your comments will likely be well received and will go far toward establishing meaningful, positive home-school relations. The investment of time will reap rewards that support more effective communication, when and if problems do develop.

WHAT TO DO?

Develop a repertoire of schoolwide practices for sharing positives with parents.

- Make weekly evening calls to at least five parents simply to convey a positive thought or compliment regarding their child.
- Write positive notes in homework planners.
- Send positive e-mail messages.

- Supply positive postcards for use in classrooms that can be used by students and adults.
- Create positive Web site features.
- Encourage staff appearances at children's activities and special events after hours.

5.6—HOW EFFECTIVE ARE DETENTIONS?

Some school staffs feel a necessity to institute an afterschool detention policy for students that perpetually fail to abide by rules or meet minimum expectations. But how effective are detentions? Are they worth the hassle to parents and staff?

Commonly, just a few teachers generate a majority of detention referrals. Moreover, typically those same teachers rarely have responsibility for supervision of the detention room or check to see if any desired results were achieved.

For some students, a detention can produce positive outcomes. Those students often have parents who assume parenting responsibilities and initiate consequences at home that motivate a change in the child's attitude and behavior. But too many other children don't have that support. For them, a detention is not effective. The experience becomes a source of frustration and wasted time for the staff persons assigned to supervise. Unless there is a structured environment in the detention room, buy-in from the entire staff, support from a majority of parents, and several viable alternative plans that can be used when students and parents can't serve or absolutely refuse a detention, long-term effectiveness of detentions is unlikely.

Detentions, when they work best, are handled *the same day by the referring teacher with parent support.* Otherwise, the worry and frustration created when a child is not picked up after detention, the strain upon communication and relationships with parents, the frequent challenges to teacher authority, and unchanged behavior outweigh any short-term benefits.

Are detentions your last-resort solutions? When tempted to issue a detention, step back, gain composure, buy time, and dig deeper to discover what really motivates the child's inappropriate actions. Ask the "why" question at least five times. Hopefully, you'll arrive at the source of the problem and a better response and solution will be very obvious.

5.7—ELIMINATE CLUTTER
THROUGHOUT THE CAMPUS

Some packrats would benefit from a rule such as, "if you haven't used it in two years, throw it away." They increasingly collect materials and supplies within undersized classrooms. Eventually, storage cabinets, media and art carts, volunteer cubicles, and the like begin appearing in the hallways and every nook within the school. Teachers sometimes bring far too many personal items to school like popcorn makers, microwaves, refrigerators, fans, radios, plants, aquariums, and so forth that take up limited space. In extreme cases, the fire inspector might object and demand order.

Teachers' classrooms are not the only location for clutter. File cabinets should be emptied of unnecessary papers annually. Teacher work rooms, staff lounges, and office storage should receive a thorough cleaning more than once each year.

Students can be organized into teams to assist with cleaning the school grounds; they'll love it and work hard to please. At the same time, they can develop a sense of pride in their school and neighborhood. Have them plant flowers—you may be surprised at the number of students who have never had their hands in dirt.

Want to know a common location of the dirtiest, most cluttered area of the school? Peek in the staff lounge. And for a real surprise, open the staff refrigerator door after about six weeks of school!

5.8—ESTABLISH CURB APPEAL

If you live in an apartment or condo complex, do you rely upon others for every cleaning or gardening need? Do you pick up trash or report unlocked doors and dangerous conditions? If you have pride in where you live, you likely assume some responsibility yourself.

Imagine you are a visitor arriving at your school. What would you see? Weeds? Flowers? Broken sidewalks? Doors needing painting or cleaning? Manicured lawns? Cigarette butts everywhere? Multiple indicators of welcome, or the impersonal "Visitors Must Report to the Office" sign? When students, staff, and parents display pride in their school, it is clean and well maintained.

You may ask, is this your responsibility? Does it really affect school structure or student learning? Yes, children learn better in environments that are clean, safe, comfortable, well-lit, and welcoming. Everyone benefits when litter control becomes a schoolwide standard. Children must be taught to respect others' property, and certainly that of the school. Little things add up and contribute to good curb appeal and cleanliness, such as picking up scrap paper from the floor. Positive behavior reinforcement and supervision take less time than removing gum from the bottom of chairs, scrubbing pencil marks from walls, or sanding carvings etched into desks and chairs.

If your school is old, in a decaying neighborhood, lacking resources, or in other ways inadequate, it should still be cleaned and receive basic care and maintenance. Read Malcolm Gladwell's analysis of the theory of broken windows in his bestseller, *The Tipping Point* (Gladwell, 2000), and visualize the similarities of positive change that can be realized when minor repairs, such as Gladwell's example of fixing broken windows in ghettos, can reduce negative behavior.

First impressions are difficult to erase. Don't allow visitors to acquire doubts about your school before they even get inside.

> **Few, if any of us, will ever receive a standing ovation or an accolade of any sort for our diligent and competent attention to facilities management. Still, we know how important this work is to facilitate a conducive learning environment for all students in our schools.**
>
> —Jeffrey Glanz (2006)

5.9—ELIMINATE GUM

Many principals, at the request of their custodians, consider this expectation to be nonnegotiable. If you question why, join the custodial staff as they work to remove dried gum from carpet or from underneath chairs during summer cleaning. That should help justify this schoolwide rule for anyone in doubt.

Moreover, chewing gum while teaching seems to violate the rules of etiquette. Set a positive example for children.

5.10—PREPARE THE CLASSROOM FOR CUSTODIAN CLEANING

Evening custodians are likely to be able to gauge the effectiveness of teachers' classroom management simply by the condition in which individuals' rooms are left after school. Those rooms where litter covers the floor, desks are overflowing with books and papers (especially the teacher's), chairs are scattered around the room (some upside down), and equipment is never turned off become a cleaning challenge for the most talented custodial staff. Rooms such as these require extra time and effort to clean, and custodians have reason to question the management abilities of the teacher.

Teaching staffs should adhere to a common standard for preparing their classrooms for daily cleaning, and principals set the tone. Students will benefit from the daily discipline of organizing and attention to detail. Moreover, clean classrooms are less prone to outbreaks of communicable disease.

Teaching children to pick up after themselves is a valuable life lesson. The simple act of clearing the classroom might transfer into more widespread awareness of environmental cleanliness and create a better community in which to live and work.

5.11—ESTABLISH PROCEDURES FOR DETERMINING STUDENT CLASSROOM PLACEMENTS

As one academic year ends, principals begin planning for the next. Classroom assignments are commonly determined in late May before the end of the school year.

In some schools, the process of assigning students to classrooms remains solely the principal's task. Parent or guardian input is not requested. Parents and students are expected to accept whatever placement decision is made. However, times have changed and choice is becoming more and more a common part of the school culture.

What better form of parental involvement can there be than developing a high level of comfort and respect between parents and teachers as placements are made? When parents are permitted to make a wise, informed decision and request a teacher that will challenge and best meet the needs of their child, the potential for involvement and success is greatly improved.

Increasingly, principals and teachers are encouraging parents to participate in the decision-making process regarding classroom placement decisions. However, from the beginning, one guideline must be made clear. Classroom placement decisions are an opportunity to develop learning environments for optimal achievement, not social networks. Then, within preestablished parameters, do what works best for students and families. Monitor the balance of race, gender, ethnicity, and academic potential and achievement of all students.

It can be a rough year for a teacher if a parent doesn't want his or her child in that teacher's class. Don't ignore past history and experience.

Gather as much information as you can. Likewise, teachers need to have input into the decisions. They know each other's strengths and weaknesses and most often will work to create equity in class assignments.

Parents will appreciate the invitation to participate in this major decision. Devoting time and thought to managing and structuring win-win scenarios for all constituents will make your school more inclusive.

> **In a great teacher's classroom, every student feels like the favorite.**
>
> —Todd Whitaker (Whitaker & Lumpa, 2005)

5.12—REFLECT AND TAKE ACTION ON IMPORTANT ISSUES

Before going home for the day, take time to reflect on all that transpired. If you are a teacher and you sense any anxiety about an interaction or encounter with a student, parent, or volunteer that might result in a call to the principal, tell him or her about it, send an explanatory e-mail, or leave a note before you go home. Principals should follow the same practice, alerting the superintendent or other superior of potentially tough issues *before* a parent or community member makes contact with him or her.

This is simply a courteous practice that can solidify your support, assuming your actions were appropriate, and help your superiors better understand both sides to an issue and defend your actions. It is not good practice for the boss to hear complaints and learn of problems from others. Everyone makes mistakes, and even the most veteran staff member can occasionally be blindsided by a developing issue. Just make it a practice to reflect, be aware of others' perceptions, and keep all your bases covered. It's those staff who appear to be clueless that are most difficult to support and place the administrator in the most tenuous of positions.

Here is a sample of reflective questions that might be considered each day:

- What lessons were most effective and well received and what strategies helped students achieve success?
- What procedures, rules, or guidelines might need to be reinforced with students or retaught to achieve better results?
- What might the entire staff need to discuss and improve to support the structures of safety, supervision, student welfare, or motivation?

5.13—BE A MASTER MOTIVATOR

Can teachers learn to be master motivators as well as excellent instructional leaders? Yes, everyone can develop his or her personal characteristics and exceed expectations. When professionals all focus their efforts in this way and share best practices, positive results will occur.

WHAT TO DO?

Consider these suggestions for thinking and behaving in ways that motivate children and adults.

- Be generous with your praise of others.
- Make sure your integrity is above reproach.
- Expect the best and work continuously to achieve positive results.
- Maintain your content knowledge and instructional skills so they are second to none.
- Continuously establish clear and achievable goals.
- Look for others' strengths and good qualities instead of focusing on their weaknesses.
- Keep an open mind and be willing to change.
- Have a vision of what you hope to achieve and make sure that others can see themselves in that same future. Get out front and pull others with you rather than pushing them. Make sure you have purpose and direction in everything you do.
- Listen to people and actually hear what they say.
- Provide caring, sincere, and confident feedback. Mean what you say! Don't be two-faced.
- Cooperate and collaborate with others.
- Ask questions and clarify what you don't understand.
- Show people that you have a genuine, warm personality and that you care.
- Demonstrate continuous energy and vitality.
- Show enthusiasm for learning and mastering new skills.
- Become an articulate speaker and writer.
- Practice what you preach. Set a personal example that will attract others who want to work hard, achieve excellence, exceed your goals, and surpass their own possibilities.

Don't complain that students lack motivation. If that's what you think, take a long look in the mirror and determine if the reflection you see is of a person you would be excited to follow. If what you see is less than positive, then you've got some changing to do. Remember, everyone can improve skills and learn to motivate others. Those who do it best are continuously working to find ways to be even better. It is most desirable when the entire staff works and learns together.

5.14—COORDINATE LEARNING OPPORTUNITIES WITH THE AFTERSCHOOL PROGRAM

Afterschool programs are widespread, with nearly two-thirds of the nation's principals reporting some type of program associated with their school (NAESP, 2001). Clearly, the endorsement and support of the principal is the key to developing the vision and mission of school-based afterschool programs (NAESP, 2006). With ever-increasing add-ons and mandates, there simply isn't adequate time to cover all requirements, especially for at-risk children in need of extra time to catch up. To maximize learning opportunities and provide quality care for children during the high-risk hours between three and six o'clock, quality afterschool programs can be a win-win for everyone.

However, program effectiveness is often limited by space and turf issues. Students fail to benefit from optimal learning opportunities when communication breaks down between the school staff and afterschool personnel. The principal has the power and influence to make sure that doesn't happen. Effective teachers know that periodic visits to the afterschool program can further motivate the students and afterschool staff. Those visits also enable teachers to get a firsthand observation of opportunities for learning extension.

Developing strong links between schools and community-based afterschool programs creates good relations and can result in partnerships that support the entire school community. Without a doubt, the time invested to orchestrate and support what happens for children after school, in whatever location, just makes good sense.

Principals need to help teachers see the connections—afterschool helps students do better in the school.

Tom Archuleta, principal (quoted in NAESP, 2006)

CONCLUDING THOUGHTS

The typical school year becomes a whirlwind of activities: answering students' questions, teaching classes, going to meetings, conferencing, observing, and engaging in phone conversations and interactions with people. Time flies. No wonder people are tired at the end of a day and need a summer break at the end of a school year! Yet remember, the end of the day or year is an important time to teach and reinforce positive behaviors.

It is important to recognize the value of having a life and interests away from school. Structure your day and allow time for *you*. Avoid burnout. Exercise, visit friends, volunteer at a nursing home, read, shop—do something that helps draw you away from the stressors that have accumulated throughout the day. Enjoy a hobby. Take care of yourself. Get enough rest for the next day.

Don't forget to maintain a good sense of humor. What might have seemed so critical or important today will likely be lighter or even funny tomorrow and months from now. Shake off the problems and stress. Laugh, smile, and enjoy your family and time at home.

> **The greatest danger for most of us is not that our aim is too high and we will miss it, but that it is too low and we will reach it.**
>
> —Michelangelo

Checklist 5—Endings: Structural Analysis and Assessment

(See explanation of the structural analysis and assessment checklists at the end of Chapter 1.)

Goal	Indicators	Master Level	Professional Level	Inconsistent Level	Ineffective Level	Not Observable
1. There is evidence of planning for a safe and orderly dismissal.	• All staff members assume responsibility for supervision of assigned students to designated areas. • Students are dismissed to parent or guardian and transfer is documented. • Accommodations for bus riders are a priority. • Drop-off locations at bus stops are safe and supervised. • Students that walk home are safe and supervised. • Safety considerations for everyone at dismissal are observable. • Staff members ride buses. • Teachers are aware of where students live. • Clutter is nonexistent.					
2. Detentions are well planned.	• Parent communication has taken place and support gained. • Detentions are planned to positively change student behaviors. • Problems are reported to appropriate officials before the end of the day.					
3. Staff interaction with parents, bus drivers, and afterschool personnel is positive.	• School-to-home communication with parents is positive. • Preventative problem solving is observed. • Attention is given to customer service. • Teachers walk students home and make positive phone calls.					
4. Teachers and paraprofessionals interact and communicate with students and parents in a positive manner.	• A code of conduct is reinforced. • A sense of order, consistency, and cooperation among staff is observable. • There is a plan for determining schedules and student classroom placements that is supported by parents and teachers.					

(Continued)

(Continued)

Summary Notes:

Identified Norms of School Structure:

Areas of Strength:

Targeted Areas for Improvement:

Adult Behavioral Norms Needed to Achieve Expectations:

Recommendations:

Summary Comments

Whether alone or reading and sharing this book with others, hopefully you have reflected and envisioned your school setting and discovered new ideas or stumbled upon an "aha!" insight or two that will make your school a better place to work and learn. It was never this author's intention to complete a comprehensive volume that would address every structural issue that may present itself in every school. That would be impractical and most likely impossible. But you might spend some time considering items not discussed here, such as homework help lines, automated phone systems, Web sites, school-based health clinics, uniforms, and weekend food grab bags, that might be appropriate for your school. Brainstorm with colleagues and you'll develop many more. Your school will be better for the effort.

No matter if you are a college student, a student teacher, substitute, or even a veteran staff member, the advice presented within each chapter and specific essays is intended to help you, the professional working toward continuous improvement and best practice, establish for yourself and your colleagues what must be defined and structured in *your* school, then taught and continuously reinforced—by the entire professional staff—for the production of a safe, secure, inclusive, welcoming, efficient, and effective learning environment. Best wishes to you as you proceed in creating just that!

> A proactive management plan, supported consistently each day, by all staff, will foster a safe, caring environment; direction and limits for students; support for adults; and minimal stress and uncertainty for the entire school community.

**Taking charge of what we can change does work,
and it works spectacularly.**

—Robert DiGiulio (2000)

The bottom line is that your customers and employees are going to have an emotional experience because of their contact with your organization, whether they like it or not. Your responsibility—and challenge—is to provide them with the kind of emotional connection that will inspire loyalty.

—Scott McKain (2002)

Recommended Readings

American college dictionary. (1967). New York: Random House.

benShea, N. (2000). *What every principal would like to say . . . and what to say next time.* Thousand Oaks, CA: Corwin Press.

Boult, B. (2006). *176 ways to involve parents* (2nd ed.). Thousand Oaks, CA: Corwin Press.

Boynton, M., & Boynton, C. (2005). *The educator's guide to preventing and solving discipline problems.* Alexandria, VA: Association for Supervision and Curriculum Development.

Brady, K., Forton, M., Porter, D., & Wood, C. (2003). *Rules in school.* Turners Falls, MA: Northeast Foundation for Children.

Breaux, A., & Wong, H. (2003). *New teacher induction: How to train, support, and retain new teachers.* Mountain View, CA: Harry K. Wong Publications.

Brinkman, R., & Kirschner, R. (2006). *Dealing with difficult people.* New York: McGraw-Hill.

Deasy, R. (Ed.). (2002). *Critical links: Learning in the arts and student academic and social development.* Washington, DC; Arts Education Partnership.

Denton, P., & Kriete, R. (2000). *The first six weeks of school.* Turners Falls, MA: Northeast Foundation for Children.

Dietz, W. (1998). Childhood weight affects adult morbidity and mortality. *The Journal of Nutrition, 128*(2), 411S–414S.

DiGiulio, R. (2000). *Positive classroom management: A step-by-step guide to successfully running the show without destroying student dignity* (2nd ed.). Thousand Oaks, CA: Corwin Press.

Drucker, P. (2001). *The essential Drucker.* New York: HarperCollins.

DuFour, R. (1991). *The principal as staff developer.* Bloomington, IN: National Educational Service.

Duke, D. (2004). The turnaround principal: High-stakes leadership. *Principal, 84*(1), 12–23.

Gardner, H. (1993). *Frames of mind: The theory of multiple intelligences.* New York: Basic Books.

Gladwell, M. (2000). *The tipping point.* New York: Little, Brown.

Glanz, J. (2006). *What every principal should know about operational leadership.* Thousand Oaks, CA: Corwin Press.

Gordon, G. (2006). *Building engaged schools: Getting the most out of America's classrooms.* New York: Gallup Press.

Greene, M. (1995). *Releasing the imagination.* San Francisco: Jossey-Bass.

Hansen, M. V., & Batten, J. (1995). *The master motivator: Secrets of inspiring leadership.* Deerfield Beach, FL: Health Communications.

Kennedy, E., & Cooney, E. (2001). Development of the child nutrition programs in the United States. *The Journal of Nutrition, 131*(2), 431S–436S.

Lindley, F. (2003). *The portable mentor.* Thousand Oaks, CA: Corwin Press.

Maxwell, J. (2002*). Leadership 101: What every leader needs to know.* Nashville, TN: Thomas Nelson.

Maxwell, J. (2003). *Ethics 101: What every leader needs to know.* New York: Warner Books.

McKain, S. (2002). *All business is show business.* Nashville, TN: Rutledge Hill Press.

National AfterSchool Association. (1998). *The NAA standards for school-age care.* Boston: Author.

National Association of Elementary School Principals. (2001). *Principals and after-school programs: A survey of preK–8 principals.* Alexandria, VA: Author.

National Association of Elementary School Principals. (2002). *Leading learning communities: Standards for what principals should know and be able to do.* Alexandria, VA: Author.

National Association of Elementary School Principals. (2005). *Leading early childhood learning communities: What principals should know and be able to do.* Alexandria, VA: Author.

National Association of Elementary School Principals. (2006). *Leading after-school learning communities: What principals should know and be able to do.* Alexandria, VA: Author.

National Center for Safe Routes to School. (n.d.). Retrieved May 4, 2007, from http://www.saferoutesinfo.org

Orlick, T. (1982). *The cooperative sports & games book.* New York: Pantheon.

Payne, R. (1996). *A framework for understanding poverty.* Highlands, TX: aha! Process.

Sigford, J. (2006). *The effective school leader's guide to management.* Thousand Oaks, CA: Corwin Press.

Stronge, J. (2002). *Qualities of effective teachers.* Alexandria, VA: Association for Supervision and Curriculum Development.

United States Department of Agriculture. (2006). The school breakfast program. *Fact sheet.* Retrieved March 3, 2007, from http://www.fns.usda.gov/cnd/breakfast/AboutBFast/SBPFactSheet.pdf

Warner, C., & Curry, M. (1997). *Everybody's house—the schoolhouse.* Thousand Oaks, CA: Corwin Press.

Whitaker, T., & Lumpa, D. (2005). *Great quotes for great educators.* Larchmont, NY: Eye of Education.

Wood, C. (1999). *Time to teach, time to learn.* Turners Falls, MA: Northeast Foundation for Children.

Wood, G. (1992). *Schools that work.* New York: Penguin Books.

Young, P. (2004). *You have to go to school, you're the principal! 101 tips to make it better for your students, your staff, and yourself.* Thousand Oaks, CA: Corwin Press.

Young, P., Sheets, J., & Knight, D. (2005). *Mentoring principals.* Thousand Oaks, CA: Corwin Press.

Index

NAESP

NATIONAL ASSOCIATION OF ELEMENTARY SCHOOL PRINCIPALS

Serving All Elementary and Middle Level Principals